THE
AGE
OF
OVER
WHELM

THE AGE OF OVER WHELM

STRATEGIES FOR THE LONG HAUL

Laura van Dernoot Lipsky

BK

Berrett–Koehler Publishers, Inc.
a BK Life book

Berrett-Koehler Publishers, Inc.
1333 Broadway, Suite 1000
Oakland, CA 94612-1921
Tel: (510) 817-2277   Fax: (510) 817-2278   www.bkconnection.com

Ordering Information
Quantity sales. Special discounts are available on quantity purchases by corporations, associations, and others. For details, contact the "Special Sales Department" at the Berrett-Koehler address above.
Individual sales. Berrett-Koehler publications are available through most bookstores. They can also be ordered directly from Berrett-Koehler:
Tel: (800) 929-2929; Fax: (802) 864-7626; www.bkconnection.com.
Orders for college textbook/course adoption use. Please contact Berrett-Koehler:
Tel: (800) 929-2929; Fax: (802) 864-7626.

Distributed to the U.S. trade and internationally by Penguin Random House Publisher Services.

Berrett-Koehler and the BK logo are registered trademarks of Berrett-Koehler Publishers, Inc.

Printed in Canada.

Berrett-Koehler books are printed on long-lasting acid-free paper. When it is available, we choose paper that has been manufactured by environmentally responsible processes. These may include using trees grown in sustainable forests, incorporating recycled paper, minimizing chlorine in bleaching, or recycling the energy produced at the paper mill.

Credits: Cartoons appearing on pages 2, 6, 8, 17, 19, 21, 22, 27, 30, 34, 35, 38, 40, 43, 46, 49, 51, 53, 57, 58, 62, 66, 68, 72, 75, 79, 87, 92, 95, 97, 100, 102, 106, 108, 110, 112, 122, 126, 130, 136, 137, and 144 are all copyrighted to The New Yorker Collection. Licensed by Cartoonbank.com. All Rights Reserved. The cartoon appearing on page 30 is copyrighted and licensed to Bob Mankoff. All Rights Reserved. The poem on page 127 is by Thich Nhat Hanh, © Plum Village Community of Engaged Buddhism, Inc.

Library of Congress Cataloging-in-Publication Data
Names: Lipsky, Laura van Dernoot, author.
Title: Overwhelmed : strategies for the long haul / Laura Van Dernoot Lipsky.
Description: Oakland, CA : Berrett-Koehler Publishers, [2018] | Includes bibliographical references and index.
Identifiers: LCCN 2018011561 | ISBN 9781523094738 (pbk.)
Subjects: LCSH: Stress management. | Distress (Psychology) | Psychology—Practice.
Classification: LCC RA785 .L573 2018 | DDC 155.9/042—dc23
LC record available at https://lccn.loc.gov/2018011561

First Edition
26 25 24 23 22 21 20 19 18   10 9 8 7 6 5 4 3 2

Editor: Julie McCann
Production management: Michael Bass Associates
Additional proofreading: PeopleSpeak
Book design: Julie Gallagher
Cover design: Yuko Uchikawa
Cover production: Jonita Bernstein
Cover photo: Chris Jordan

For Mikaela and Aliyah

"What do you do in times of despair?"

Archbishop Desmond Tutu was asked.

"You show your humanity."

CONTENTS

ACKNOWLEDGMENTS   xi

FOREWORD   xiii

Introduction   1

Finding a way through   3

Responding with intention   8

ONE **What Does Overwhelm Look Like?**   15

Personal overwhelm   16

Relationships and family overwhelm   20

Community and society overwhelm   22

TWO **What Causes Overwhelm?**   27

External and internal forces   28

Our commitments   40

Environment   47

THREE **A Way Through: When Less Is More**   53

Metabolizing exposure   54

Relieving saturation   55

Acknowledging potential barriers   57

When less is more   60

FOUR **Less Distraction, More Intention**   65

FIVE **Disconnect Less, Be Present More**   89

SIX Less Attachment, More Curiosity   103

SEVEN Less Depletion, More Stamina   119

EIGHT When to Step Away   143
Make informed choices   143
Question whether and how to remain   147

Conclusion   153

NOTES   157

INDEX   173

ABOUT THE AUTHOR   181

ACKNOWLEDGMENTS

My eternal gratitude to Josh and our girls for our life together, for your unwavering patience, and for your steadfast humor throughout the writing of this book. To Jeevan Sivasubramaniam for never giving up on the vision for this coming to be and for your graciousness. I am eternally grateful to Julie McCann without whom this would have not been possible and whose writing and editing skills and life insights remained a saving grace throughout. Connie Burk provided a depth of critique and well of encouragement that informed the entire process and allowed this book to go places I could only go with her. Z, for his comforting presence.

My deep appreciation for all who contributed to the evolution of this effort with such generosity and warmth: Nate, Jay, Sarah, Buddy, Mary, Robin, Lonnie, Michael, Deborah, Kelsey, Tyler, ShaKiana, Dr. Goldman, Emmett, Abby, Nikki, Maria, Steven, Grace, Billie, Sadie, Evie, Sue, Karen, Lelan, Lili, Felix, Lily, Maddy, Wanjeri, Jonah, Maddie, Noor, Lori, Maya, Tony, Renée, Lia, Maya, Ella, Min, Kate, Xavier, Hannah, Zoë, Jacob, Dina, Deb, Tripat, Michelle, Jake, Tom, Melissa, Cesar, Rob, Toby, Dr. Amy, the Lilly family, Sister Trai Nghiem, Allison, and Matthew. To Phil, Tim, Maggie, Ingrid, and Meg: Your feedback was critical and a true gift. My many thanks to Yuko, Jonita, and Chris for gracing me with the cover. Thank you to Vance, Deepa, Judge Berns, Dr. Graff, Faisal, and Françoise for your kind words. To Addison and Miriam: Thank you for your attention to detail. To *The New Yorker* cartoonists: I remain indebted to you. To Helena Brantley and the entire team at Berrett-Koehler: I so appreciate you creating this opportunity for me. Margarita and Samantha, I treasure your steady support for all this time.

To all those who have welcomed *Trauma Stewardship* into your lives throughout the years: Thank you, truly. And to each of my teachers and every person with whom I get to share this path . . . there are no words to express my abiding gratitude.

FOREWORD
by Connie Burk

I took my first lesson from Laura van Dernoot Lipsky nearly twenty years ago when I suggested that a periodic free muffin might be a sufficient expression of organizational support to her as a domestic violence advocate in my employ. In the moments and years to follow, Laura has taught me volumes about what it takes to metabolize trauma and address the toll that caring for others can take on our lives.

Her work on trauma exposure and emotional labor has transformed the discussion about fostering personal and collective well-being as an essential means to social justice ends. There is no movement, no field, no sector that has not been touched by her research, insights, and exhortations. Every week, I hear from advocates in the movement to end domestic violence who have walked themselves back from the brink of mental, spiritual, physical, and emotional collapse by following the path that Laura laid out in *Trauma Stewardship* and the work of her Institute.

In my travels connected to my long collaboration with Laura and my own work in the movements to end domestic, sexual, and state violence, I often encounter the strong conviction that idealism and pragmatism are opposite ends of one adversarial continuum. If someone seeks to stand in solidarity with global struggles for justice, innovate a technology or way of understanding the world, or assert and work toward a vision of a repaired world, that person is fixed into the idealist end of the spectrum. On the other end, we lock in the people who are considered realistic, resource-focused, no-nonsense, get-it-done types. Some people dismiss the idealist crowd as head-in-the-clouds dreamers for whom the perfect is perpetually the enemy of the good. Some people dismiss the pragmatist set as stunted and self-serving, unable to see the forest for the trees. Whether valorized or castigated, the idea persists that these approaches are necessarily antagonistic to one another—as if idealistic goals and pragmatic methods cannot exist in one person or one approach. For those of us who advance practical steps toward achieving idealistic goals, this faulty continuum is a constant pain in the ass.

Nowhere is the problem at the center of this false binary more evident than in how we think about the experience of overwhelm for ourselves and each other, as we endeavor to tackle personal or collective challenges or work to achieve our aspirations.

In this new conscientiously researched, beautifully written, hauntingly timely exhortation, Laura moves beyond trauma exposure to take on the generalized state of overwhelm engulfing so many people in our local and global communities.

The Age of Overwhelm is a signal beacon showing us how a practical accounting of our internal resources and a clear-eyed assessment of our ability to manage a sense of overwhelm are compatible with both aspirational goals—those we have for ourselves, our families, our communities, and our world—and pragmatic methods. Indeed, her instructions and reminders demonstrate how we can and must commit to resolving this tension and coming back to a sustainable center in our lives.

Laura's breadth of experience and generosity in sharing from both personal and professional realms animate the lessons to be learned in *The Age of Overwhelm*. Laura knows how to bring the full range of evidence to her offering. She distills research detailing the consequences of long states of overwhelm, then brings the contextual and experiential evidence we need to make sense of what is in or what is out of our individual control. Her analysis serves also for a meditation, and it is right on time.

For the past year, a series of signs have hung in the window of my office facing out to the street. They say: Show up. Show up. Show up.

Laura believes that we can. We can show up. We can be in it— our business, our movements, our art, our families, our schools, our neighborhoods, our spiritual practices—for the long haul. *The Age of Overwhelm* invites the dreamers and the builders, and all of those somewhere in the middle, to take up this book and get at it.

"We all carry within us our places of exile, our crimes, our ravages. Our task is not to unleash them on the world; it is to transform them in ourselves."

—Albert Camus, philosopher and author

INTRODUCTION

Though the man was seated in the middle of a room, surrounded by hundreds of colleagues, he managed to make piercing eye contact with me as he leaned slightly forward and said slowly, deliberately, and unwaveringly, "What I want from you is that I *need* to feel *completely* different than I feel right now, and I don't want to have to do *anything* about it."

He is not alone.

Although I have formally been involved in social change, social justice, environmental justice, and trauma work for more than thirty years, I am finding myself amid a landscape that is, at times, unrecognizable. Not in the content—suffering has been around for a long time, of course—but in the *depth* and *breadth* of the pain, despair, and overwhelm so many folks throughout the world are feeling. When my colleague spoke, he was surrounded by a richly diverse group of individuals representing scores of groups, organizations, and movements. And yet, every individual in that room could relate, profoundly, to what he was sharing.

What I didn't anticipate when I first started this work was that this sense of being overwhelmed would not just be a powerful undercurrent in the various fields I work in, but that it would permeate society. Individuals are overwhelmed. Families are overwhelmed. Workplaces, communities, and entire systems are overwhelmed. And while each time in history has its challenges, there is a particular look in folks' eyes today that has prompted me to dedicate this book to those who are operating in a state of overwhelm—some of the time, or all of the time.

As humans, we don't do well being overwhelmed. And if you've found your way to this book, you are likely somewhere along the continuum of feeling overwhelmed—whether you're desperate to shift something but don't think you have it in you, or you're already trying to remedy the situation and need a hand. Some of you are interested in this because your own day-to-day life feels like a lot, and your very well-being is at stake. Maybe your home life is rough, or your body is physically failing you. Some of you are drawn to this because you're in a caretaking role to family members or friends. Others of you are trying to show up and contribute in your community. Some of you are in school, and that can be, in and of itself, challenging to navigate. Some of you are trying to wrestle support, recognition, or justice out of community and state systems that, at best, are also overwhelmed. Others of you are here because of your work—either because the structure of your workplace leaves something to be desired or because what you're exposed to on the job is a lot, or both. And for some, you're feeling it on any combination of these fronts. It may even seem ubiquitous—a burgeoning sense of societal despair. No matter the cause, the sensation of overwhelm and the impact that it has on your ability to focus and make your way through the world can be disorienting or even debilitating.

"Fear and loathing about the future have shaken me to the very core of my being. What's good for that?"

For all the years I have been involved in frontline trauma work and teaching on systematic oppression and liberation theory, there is one question that has surfaced repeatedly. I have been asked this question, in only slightly different ways, by folks from around the world in workplaces ranging from small nonprofits to huge hospitals, prisons to wildlife conservation groups, political organizing offices to Ivy League universities, from Facebook to the Pentagon. It has been asked by individuals facing personal and professional challenges, family members caring for each other, veterans returning home, elected officials trying to govern, volunteers fulfilling their commitments, and clergy providing places of sanctuary. And it has been asked by countless adolescents and young adults as they try to find their way through their teen years and beyond: "What do I do?"

The answer, I think, is to do *something*. And, often, less is more. But while *The Age of Overwhelm* will strongly suggest you do *something* to help you sustain for the long haul, I assure you it does not require doing *everything* you may be dreading. My intention is not to pile tasks on to your existing to-do list, but simply to remind you that you have options. Please roll through this book in whatever way is most helpful—whether you're interested in how we got here and the potential pitfalls of overwhelm or you're seeking concrete action steps. If a section feels like too much, read the cartoons and skip ahead. And, as always, take breaks. One afternoon, months into writing, my daughters walked by and without saying a word dropped into my lap a sparkling new white pencil embossed with these words: "Check it off. Go outside."

"I know the world is bruised and bleeding, and though it is important not to ignore its pain, it is also critical to refuse to succumb to its malevolence."

—Toni Morrison, author

Finding a way through

As for *how* to navigate an abiding sense of overwhelm, let's break it down. What I have learned in my personal life, as well as from tens of thousands of colleagues throughout the years, is that it's important to pay attention to what's in our control, what's not in our control, and how to tend to this reality—*practically*—in such a way as to mitigate harm, cultivate our ability to be decent and equitable, and act with integrity.

Of course, everything is connected. I have had the great privilege to be a student of Zen Master Thich Nhat Hanh. One of the things he talks about consistently is the nature of interbeing: that all things are connected, deeply. In ways big and small, we are all responsible for contributing to systemic change where change is due. There is plenty of heavy lifting to be done. But to contribute effectively—to have a foundation to manage that at all and to sustain ourselves for the long haul—we *must* tend to our own selves in parallel.

We simply can't contribute skillfully and do our best work toward effecting external changes if we aren't also taking care of the place where overwhelm takes root: within ourselves. It is also within ourselves that we have the most agency, authority, and power to change. While writing this book, I met with Dr. Robin Goldman at the University of Wisconsin. When I asked her what she was currently most inspired about, in terms of all their neuroscience research, she paused and said, "That we have the capacity to change."

What's in or out of our control

The more we feel overwhelm starting to set in, the more focused and diligent we need to be with ourselves in having a plan. When we're overwhelmed, we must, *must* determine how to metabolize and internally transform whatever is arising within us. Otherwise, it erodes us, or we cause external harm, or both. As poet and activist Audre Lorde wrote, "Caring for myself is not self-indulgence, it is self-preservation, and that is an act of political warfare." Change starts with two considerations:

- What is in our collective control?
- What is in my individual control?

It is within the bounds of our collective control to make sweeping changes to labor conditions, environmental restoration, supports for families, and more. Collective control requires large-scale learning and organizing, including the realms we think of as political—that is how we negotiate among competing interests and understandings in societies. Democracy is one answer to collective control. But as my friend and comrade Connie Burk says, "We have to have our shit together enough in our individual control arena to show up effectively for the collective control arena."

> "The human heart is the first home of democracy. It is where we embrace our questions. Can we be equitable? Can we be generous? Can we listen with our whole beings, not just our minds, and offer our attention rather than our opinions? And do we have enough resolve in our hearts to act courageously, relentlessly, without giving up—ever—trusting our fellow citizens to join with us in our determined pursuit of a living democracy?"
>
> —Terry Tempest Williams, author and activist

There are countless things in life that are out of our individual control. Depending on our religious views, spiritual orientations, and varying philosophies, our perspective on this will differ—and whether that which is out of our control is comforting or anxiety-producing will also differ. But most folks agree that a lot of things are out of our control in life. It can be helpful to start by just acknowledging this.

Sometimes, acknowledging that which is out of our individual control can be accompanied by a sense of relief, as in, "Phew! Later! Thank YOU that that's not in my control!" But often, relinquishing control is easier said than done, as some of what is not in our control can be absolutely excruciating. In that case, we can focus on: What can I do in this instance to eliminate or mitigate harm? And further, and of utmost importance, what can I do that would be helpful?

*"Pillows for sleeping on are downstairs.
These are all for screaming into."*

Then there are all the things in life that *are* in our control. At some point in my career, I shifted the focus of a central question I ask when working in the community from "How do you feel affected by your work and by your life?" to "What would your loved ones want me to know? What would they say it's like to be in a relationship with you?" I always assure folks that we can all agree anything their loved ones say are, you know, surely without evidence. I urge them to just tell me what the allegations are. No matter how quiet the group might be for the first question, folks are never quiet when I ask the second. In part, I think as humans we can become hyper-focused on what is out of our individual control, but our loved ones can frequently help us clarify, "Yes, and, even so . . . here's what's still on you and here's the collateral damage on us." While I was working with a group of police, the officers described what had become hard and overwhelming about their work. A few disclosed some things they'd noticed and then, after a pause, one officer shared, "My wife said to me recently, 'You know . . . I didn't *marry* an asshole . . . but now, here we are.'"

"People travel to wonder at the height of mountains, at the huge waves of the sea, at the long courses of rivers, at the vast

compass of the ocean, at the circular motion of the stars . . .
and they pass by themselves without wondering."

—Saint Augustine of Hippo, theologian and philosopher

Objectively acknowledging factors that are in our control may be tough, especially in situations that seem to shift by the minute or the hour. We may have some "big feelings," as we say in early childhood education, and it may require a balance of forthright honesty and kindness toward oneself to bring our insight into focus. Regardless of how we feel about circumstances within our control, and our history of navigating those circumstances, we mustn't let discomfort distract us. Psychologist Dr. Rick Hanson tells us, "The ancient emotion centers in the brain get about a two second head start over the more recent logical centers, so buy yourself some time for all the resources inside your head to come online."

Refining our ability to navigate our instincts and reconcile what would be constructive is a lifelong process, and one that is found through traditions around the world. But it doesn't take a lifetime to develop a strategy. I remember feeling embarrassed for myself with how much more skilled my daughter was at successfully dealing with this pull between feeling deeply and yet still acting well. It was in the middle of a full family heated moment with a lot of momentum when we heard her incredibly young voice say, "I just need a minute." We all stopped. She didn't go anywhere; she didn't do anything visibly. She was so young I'm not sure she could have even articulated how she recalibrated—but she did, and we did, and the rest of the discussion was much more . . . civil. As my girls have moved into their teen years, it's easier to see the ways they balance how they're feeling about their current situation with what would be constructive by taking a second and reaching for a half-eaten snack from their backpack, rolling down the car window, or walking over to pet their dog. They help me remember something central to this discussion of overwhelm: Regardless of what we're up against, and despite how we feel about our current circumstances, it's still on us to conduct ourselves appropriately. And if we haven't quite yet, we need to pause and start now.

Kanin

"You have a lot of boring health issues, so I'm prescribing medical marijuana for myself."

Responding with intention

Sometimes responding with intention takes a millisecond, and sometimes honing a healthy response takes years, but we return time and again to the reality that we have choices we *get to* or are *obligated to* make. [Choose your mood: You can take this on voluntarily or begrudgingly.] While societal pressures, our responsibilities, and the context of our lives influence us to a great extent, we still ultimately get to decide, for our part, how we are going to think, speak, and act in each moment. And those billions of moments—which unfurl and become our life, as we've learned from so many ancestors and giants on whose shoulders we stand—those tiny or grand moments of making a choice for ourselves (and, at times, on behalf of our family or our people) are what contribute to our liberation over time. As writer Joan Didion says, "The willingness to accept responsibility for one's own life—is the source from which self-respect springs."

Once we have identified circumstances within our individual control that are contributing to overwhelm, we get to ask ourselves:

- Am I going to choose to roll on as is, or should I change my circumstances? (Understanding, of course, that either way, I am accountable for the consequences.)
- What can I do in this instance to eliminate or mitigate harm?
- What can I do that would be helpful?

I so appreciated how my neighbor's boss handled one such moment. The Gates Foundation provides a year of parental leave, and my neighbor has a big job there with countless responsibilities. When it came time to tell her boss that she was pregnant, she shared the news and gave him the expected timing of when she would be taking her year away from the office. He listened, looked down, took a long inhale and a slow exhale, then looked back up, reengaged eye contact, smiled, and said sincerely, "Congratulations. I am so happy for you."

It's indescribably powerful and dignity-preserving to focus on what one can do instead of what one can't do. Author Malcolm Gladwell tells the story of Vernon Jordan and other civil rights attorneys who experienced bigotry and ongoing demeaning treatment as they stayed in Georgia, day after day, trying to defend a young black man in 1961. Each day during lunch, they ate bologna sandwiches in their car outside the courthouse, while the judge, opposing lawyers, and court officials dined in the whites-only restaurant on the square. One day, Vernon Jordan was waved down in the courthouse vestibule by a quiet woman who beckoned him to forgo the bologna and come to her house for lunch instead. She and her neighbors set the table with an elaborate feast. And according to Vernon Jordan, as the woman's husband said grace, he said, "Lord, way down here in Tattnall County, we can't join the NAACP, but thanks to your bountiful blessings, we can feed the NAACP lawyers."

Any choice is limited by the options available. And even as we work (or don't work) to make the options more equitable, more humane, more just, or more accessible, we are making choices along the way. As labor leader and civil rights activist Dolores Huerta said, "Every moment is an organizing opportunity, every person a potential activist, every minute a chance to change the world." There is merit in remembering that there can be a tension among the choices we make. There may be internal *and* external consequences. We may choose to do something that may mitigate internal harm, but that, of course, doesn't mean others will agree or understand or even respect our decisions. I imagine we can all call up one or two times in our lives when we exerted our personal agency in a situation that was, indeed, self-preserving or self-respecting and did not cause harm to anyone else. But even so, someone found our decision to be burdensome or experienced it as an affront to our relationship or their perception of us. In these times, it can be helpful to take the long view. Don't watch the ripples on the surface of the water; watch the still depths.

As we become fluent in cultivating our personal agency, we see how careful navigation can aid in keeping overwhelm at arm's length or allowing the heavy cloak to shape-shift from debilitating overwhelm, to just—you know—a drag. But even if life circumstances remain overwhelming, we can learn to coexist with them without we ourselves becoming overwhelmed. And that matters: overwhelm walking beside you versus overwhelm binding and gagging you.

The personal accounts of countless Apartheid and Holocaust survivors, prisoners of war, and survivors of torture remind us that while much can be taken from us by outside circumstances, we can always seek to preserve our deepest sense of self. As a young child, Noor Ebrahim from Cape Town, South Africa, bore witness as his home and community were literally leveled. Noor lived in the District Six community of Cape Town, which welcomed immigrants, merchants, freed slaves, laborers, and artisans. He was the fourth generation in their family home. But one of the innumerable, deplorable acts of Apartheid in the 1960s and 1970s was to forcibly remove more than 60,000 people—and District Six was flattened by bulldozers. Now, almost 40 years later, Noor works at the District Six Museum to help educate visitors about the atrocities that happened there. As he described his story to me, we were standing in front of a floor-to-ceiling display created entirely from salvaged street signs. Noor explained that the Apartheid nationalist government had given strict orders for everything to be destroyed and nothing salvaged in District Six. But one demolition foreman, while forced to follow through on the government's orders, secretly collected sign after sign until he had done everything within his ability to save all he could. After hiding the signs in his basement for years, the man donated them as a reminder both of the pain of cruelty as well as the courage of conviction—honoring the dignity of fellow South Africans.

For some survivors, preserving a deep sense of self means holding on to the joy of giving to others. For others it means never losing a sense of humor. And others have talked about not letting hate, even toward one's captors, creep in. The stories of their survival show how generosity, delight, and compassion are integral to preserving a sense of self. Then, of course, there are *our* accounts. When I am asked, "What do you do?" I've learned to be very vague. On one trip, when a particularly persistent cab driver inquired enough to find out about the work I do, he shared with me about his very abusive father and the legacy of pain brought on to the entire extended family at his father's hands. At one point, he paused and said, "All you can feel for a guy like that is compassion."

> "I don't believe any longer that we can afford to say that it is entirely out of our hands. We made the world we're living in and we have to make it over."
>
> —James Baldwin, writer

Creating conditions

To continue to show up and sustain—on any level—will require a dedicated practice of metabolizing and transforming that which is arising within us. And again, edifying ourselves in the face of overwhelm with undergirding intentions of both: How can I refrain from causing harm? And, how can I contribute—to whatever I choose—skillfully and wisely? This is a reckoning that deserves to be done daily.

In Buddhist traditions, this is sometimes taught as *creating conditions*. So even when things are out of our individual or collective control originally—and always when things are in our control—the teachings urge us to create conditions to alleviate suffering and contribute toward right speech, right conduct, right action. To be able to bring our A-game, we must continue to reach for, and inhabit where possible, some equanimity. As Sufi poet Hafiz wrote, "Act great. My dear, always act great."

> "However painful our experiences may be, they are just painful experiences until we add the response of aversion or hatred. This insight is a reversal of the ordinary way we perceive life. 'Usually,' says Ajahn Chah, 'we believe outer problems attack us.' Only then does suffering arise. If we react with hatred and aversion, these qualities become habitual. Like a distorted autoimmune response, our misguided reaction of hatred does not protect us; rather, it becomes the cause of our continued unhappiness.
>
> In a healthy response to pain and fear, we establish awareness . . . We can train ourselves to notice the gap between the moments of sense experience and the subsequent response. We can enter the space between instinct and action, between impulse and reaction."
>
> —Jack Kornfield, author and teacher

In the following chapters we'll dive deeper into the elements contributing to overwhelm: those we don't have individual control over, those we do, and what to do about it all, regardless. When I think about the various layers causing stress and strain for folks individually and collectively—locally, nationally, and internationally—they include everything from epigenetics, our health, and systematic and intergenerational oppression and trauma to relationships (with our families, community, school, and work) and our environment (the economy, the climate crisis, social structures, and world events). Each of these factors can contribute to the rising overwhelm within us all. And for each of these, we can ask ourselves: How am I contributing to and how am I reacting to this condition? Do I understand the toll of this condition on myself and others? And am I exacerbating the toll, helping to mitigate it, or transforming it?

"These days, people seem to be perpetually gearing themselves up for the epic battle of merely existing. At the end of the day, jogging up to our front doors, we are all Rocky, reaching the summit, conquering that last step: 'Just a man / and his will / to survive!' We rip our headphones off, triumphantly. We did it! Another day closer to death!"

—Amanda Petrusich, journalist and author

I have found in my life and work that there is a tender balance between the relief that can come from being acknowledged, affirmed, and validated and the very real need—that at times can feel urgent or dire—to move beyond commiseration and empathy to have a realistic plan of action. Validation may be an essential piece of understanding the toll these conditions take, and yet efficacy—actually doing something about whatever it is we're struggling with—often brings the most satisfying relief. Many may feel tension here, or perhaps even a contradiction, even though there isn't one inherently. In my experience, there is a continuous oscillation between pausing, noticing, taking something in, and finding a way through. We must consider an order of precedence, perhaps. A way through is not meant to numb us as we clip through a list of action steps or lose ourselves in everything that needs to get done. Cutting ourselves some slack can, at times, be what's most helpful, and understanding that being and doing are not mutually exclusive—though doing mindfully is not for the faint of heart.

My friend Jay Ward speaks poignantly about this, describing how piercing moments of agony stretched into days and weeks—expanding and contracting in a world turned upside down—in the aftermath of his brother's murder. Adam Ward, a TV news cameraman, and his colleague, a reporter, were killed in a malicious, horrific shooting caught on live television. In a disturbingly short amount of time, individuals, advocacy organizations, and the media began pursuing Jay and his family, hoping they would step into a public arena they did not choose nor wish to inhabit—all while Jay and his family tried desperately to make sense of the tragedy. In the days, weeks, and years since losing his brother, Jay has felt both compelled to protect his (and his family's) space to privately grieve, while also publicly advocating for gun safety. They continue to navigate that tender, painful place of being and doing.

You may be able to relate to Jay's experience, even if you have not lived through something of this magnitude. As humans, this fluid state between "What is happening?" and "How do I deal?" is likely familiar to us all. Over the years, I have walked alongside many people who have persisted in the face of deep adversity, even tragedy. People who've pulled their consciousness together in the wake of both chronic challenges and acute heartbreak. In this book I share their stories—with deep respect—and share my observations of emerging patterns and practices to inform lessons we may all glean and what we can do, concretely, in the face of overwhelm.

While, you can imagine, this could be a multivolume book exploring all the ways to navigate overwhelm, we recognize that most people feel short on time, resources, and capacity. So the book itself (like the content within) is guided by a "less is more" framework. For all that is omitted . . . I apologize. I also acknowledge that most, if not all, of the contents of this book may be known to you already. As author Ursula K. Le Guin says, "Expression is not revelation."

ONE

What Does Overwhelm Look Like?

"Your chances of becoming an alcoholic are higher. You are more likely to get divorced. Chances are you will contemplate, attempt, or commit suicide."

Bullshit. That was my immediate reaction as the risks of trauma exposure in my new career were spelled out in a classroom at the state police academy. Not me. Maybe that quiet guy in the next row, but not me. I had my shit together. Period.

I graduated the basic police course at the top of my class, worked hard on the road, and after a couple of years landed a special team assignment. I was on a roll. Then I stopped at the grocery store.

It was my Friday night and I was ready to start my weekend. I would stop at the store to grab a bag of chips and my favorite beer. Three minutes tops. As I walked toward the Ten Items or Less express lane, a man pushing a cart slid in front of me. Slight delay, but no big deal. At least until I counted the items in his cart.

You motherfucker. There are twelve items in your cart. Can you not read the sign? Do you not know the common rules of our society? You are fucking with my timeline. Breathe. Just breathe and let it go. Wait . . . did you just pull out a fat stack of coupons and start slowly searching through them? You unbelievable asshole. I fantasize that you pull a gun on the cashier and demand the money in the register. Green light. In one smooth motion I drop my beer, lift my shirt, and draw the Glock from my right hip. I put two tightly grouped rounds into your temple from close range and watch you drop, lifeless, to the floor.

I sat in my car for a good ten minutes before I could drive. My hands were trembling with rage. My mind felt strangely satisfied with the execution fantasy. I had lost my shit. Over twelve items in a shopping cart.

Now? I have spent more than my fair share of time inside a whiskey bottle, and my marriage ended one month shy of our 25th anniversary. I have never contemplated, much less attempted, suicide. But I can't call bullshit on the possibility anymore.

—Deputy Sheriff

The state of overwhelm has many shades. It is a continuum. But many of us are, in fact, experiencing some degree of overwhelm as a natural response to all that we encounter—whether we experience that as an occasional flutter of doubt, more frequent flooding of emotion, or gripping despair that we carry with us throughout our days. In an essay on the Chinese dissident Xu Hongci, author and journalist Evan Osnos wrote, "What is the precise moment, in the life of a country, when tyranny takes hold? It rarely happens in an instant; it arrives like twilight, and, at first, the eyes adjust." So, too, is the slow descent of overwhelm. It comes like dusk and your eyes slowly adjust to it without at first knowing that the light is fading.

Personal overwhelm

Overwhelm can surface any number of ways in our individual selves. In a global survey conducted by *Forbes* in 2015, 14 percent of almost 3,000 people surveyed said they feel chronically overwhelmed. And according to the World Health Organization in 2017, "depression is the leading cause of ill health and disability worldwide."

"I feel tremendous pressure to frolic."

The overwhelm starts early. The condition seems especially prevalent in schools, and the never-ending refrain I hear from students I work with is, "I'm so stressed out." Unfortunately, research backs this up. In a 2017 article titled "Why Are More American Teenagers Than Ever Suffering From Severe Anxiety?" writer Benoit Denizet-Lewis described "a doubling of hospital admissions for suicidal teenagers over the last 10 years, with the highest rates occurring soon after they return to school each fall. In its annual survey of students, the American College Health Association found a significant increase—from 50 percent in 2011 to 62 percent in 2016—of undergraduates reporting 'overwhelming anxiety' in the previous year."

In the workplace, it's no better. I will never forget sitting in a staff meeting with a group I'd been asked to consult with on what may feel overwhelming about their work, and watching as a steady stream of tears ran down a young man's face. When he finally spoke, he said softly, "I feel like every day I have to kill a part of myself to do this job. Every single day."

A significant challenge of being overwhelmed individually, regardless of the cause, is how incredibly hard it can be to have or maintain awareness that you are actually overwhelmed. This would be a totally different conversation if we consistently and reliably had insight about our overwhelm, but for most of us that's not how things work. The continuum of overwhelm can range from feeling surges of overwhelm occasionally (after which you reset and move on) to spending years trying to keep your head above water. Or you may have had that experience when in an incredibly mundane moment, you have an epiphany of sorts—either realizing how overwhelmed you are or recognizing an absence of overwhelm and consequently gaining insight into how overwhelmed you have been.

That was my experience once when I leaned over to kiss my sleeping child on her cheek and had an immediate sense of, "I am not overwhelmed right now." As I stood up, the weight of how overwhelmed I'd been, for so long, descended on me. I flashed back to the afternoon my mom died when I was thirteen. I was out on the sidewalk when the incredibly kind, very cool leader of our youth group found her way to me through several others who had gathered. She first gave me a huge, not-needing-anything-from-me hug. Then she stepped back a few inches, gripped my shoulders, looked straight into my eyes, and said, "You're in shock. This is how you may feel for a while, and it's okay. This is just what happens during times like this. It's okay." That couple of minutes has stayed with me, and it's informed countless conversations I've had with others throughout the years when I have been called in to try to help someone. Interrupting isolation during a moment of acute overwhelm, or throughout the duration of ongoing overwhelm, can be a true gift. Sometimes all it takes is helping someone acknowledge that *this* is what overwhelm looks like.

Then there are times with overwhelm when, until it plays out, there's no way to know how deep it will cut. I remember sitting in a meeting with high school educators trying to organize ongoing support for a young family friend who had suddenly lost her father in an accident. We outlined action steps for hours. One after the other. And partway through the meeting, one of the educators paused, the room got quiet, and she said, "Of course, the family can't even begin to understand at this time all that they have lost."

We see this frequently with disasters, too. Of course, you know the event is catastrophic, but the evolving sense of being overwhelmed is heartrending. Alyssa Mastromonaco, former White House deputy chief of staff, spoke to this in the context of how important an effective government response is to mass overwhelm. Days after Hurricane Harvey, she said, "Right now, people are happy to be alive. They are happy to know that their families are okay. In about, I don't know, a couple days . . . any day now . . . people are just going to be like, 'Where the fuck is my shit? I want to go home!'"

"The body keeps the score: If the memory of trauma is encoded in the viscera, in heartbreaking and gut-wrenching emotions, in autoimmune disorders and skeletal/muscular problems, and if mind/brain/visceral communication is the royal road to emotion regulation, this demands a radical shift in our therapeutic assumptions. . . . . The challenge of recovery is to reestablish ownership of your body and your mind—of your self. This means feeling free to know what you know and to feel what you feel without becoming overwhelmed, enraged, ashamed, or collapsed."

—Dr. Bessel van der Kolk, founder and medical director of The Trauma Center

Raising our awareness of where we are individually on this overwhelm continuum is something we aim to do throughout this book. As one colleague shared with me, she had no idea to what degree her

"You come home to find me eating beans from a giant can. How do you think my day went?"

internal struggle was manifesting externally until her toddler said to her, "Mama, what's wrong with your face?"

I *still* am surprised by how unaware of my own overwhelm I am at times. I was once attending my daughter's basketball game and sitting in a particularly boisterous section. It was during a time when I'd been called in on several school and community shootings and was continuing to meet with those devastated by the losses. I knew I was tired, but I didn't realize how on edge I was until early in the first quarter when some of the extra loud fans started yelling, "Watch the shooter!" every *single* time someone went up for a shot. I felt my heart beat faster and heat rise within me. I tried to talk myself down and practice all the somatic grounding principles I've learned. But by the second quarter, I'd moved as far away from the game as possible while still having the court in sight. Sometimes, once our nervous system gets involved, it can be incredibly challenging to come down. I imagine lots of folks went to bed that night with three-pointers and excellent defense flashing through their consciousness. For me, it took days to lose the echo of "Watch the shooter!"

Relationships and family overwhelm

Overwhelm within our relationships and families can be challenging to assess, considering how skilled many are at portraying that our entire lives are "fine" and the extreme self-marketing campaigns that so many—consciously or unconsciously—participate in on social media. Social media is complicated, and there are countless benefits that come from all the opportunities we have to express ourselves and connect online. Even so, it can seem from the outside that everyone else's life is absolutely and completely divine, when what's happening on the inside, of course, is not as readily promoted. And there is no shortage of evidence of the increased isolation and demoralization that folks (both young and old) can feel when it appears that everyone else is out having fun on Saturday night, on vacation, in glorious relationships, or parenting the most spectacular children *ever*. Social media is not the only driver of a sense that one must perform the perfect life for outside observers. From classic pressure to keep up with the Joneses in neighborhoods or congregations to the ominous state scrutiny toward immigrants, refugees, and people living in public housing or seeking community services, the stakes for living up to external expectations can be ineffable.

"With four or more kids' meals, you get a shot of bourbon."

There have always been generational challenges, one generation to the next. According to research from The Gottman Institute, for example, "67% of couples experience a precipitous decline in relationship satisfaction in the first three years of a baby's life." And as we get older, the complexity of relationships and family life often increases. One of the most common things folks share with me when I work with groups is how impossible their lives feel as they try to balance the needs of their own lives and/or that of their children while simultaneously caretaking aging parents, struggling siblings, or other family members in need. Also, I have had the privilege of working with young people for more than three decades, and lately the extent of stress and complexity I'm witnessing envelop their relationships—with each other, family members, and other adults in their lives—is like nothing I've ever seen. For young people growing up in today's societies, man can it be rough dealing with the adults who are raising them. For some this is particularly treacherous, whether it be because your folks were born in another country than where you were born or raised or because your sexual or gender identity is in conflict with those who are raising you, leaving you feeling unsafe not just out in the world but often under the roof you're meant to share.

Community and society overwhelm

Finally, we see community and society overwhelm range from stumbling along to coming apart at the seams. Whether it's caused by environmental challenges or human-induced incidents, we cannot underestimate how affected we are when living in a community or society that is overwhelmed.

"The parking is terrible, so we decided to never do anything again."

I live in a place where the majesty of the natural world is both abundant and accessible, and environmental justice is of great interest to me. I know many people working in this field—the passion with which they approach their work is admirable, and the burden of responsibility they carry is heavy. There are groups fighting for renewable energy and sustainable food. Against ocean acidification and toxic waste.

Organizations like Outdoor Afro and The Trail Posse are publicly challenging the pop culture fabrication that people of color aren't interested in the great outdoors. For people in these communities, the weight of their life's work is heavy, leaving them susceptible to overwhelm.

Pollution is fragmenting families and communities, contributing to collective overwhelm. In Beijing, grappling with the risks of escalating pollution, families consider sending their children to boarding schools in other countries, just to give their children consistent access to clean air. Toxic levels of lead in drinking water in Flint, Michigan, has had devastating physical, developmental, and psychological impact on families in the community and has claimed a number of lives. The direct toll may not be fully understood for decades.

Lack of access to nature contributes to poor health and overwhelm in many communities. Author Richard Louv said, "Nature-deficit disorder is not a formal diagnosis, but a way to describe the psychological, physical, and cognitive costs of human alienation from nature, particularly for children in their vulnerable developing years." And according to a report from the Institute for European Environmental Policy for Friends of the Earth Europe, inequality in mental well-being is greater among people who report limited access to green areas, compared with those with good access.

Deprivation of natural environments is also a racial justice issue. In certain urban areas in the United States, residents are denied equitable services (banking, insurance, health care, or supermarkets) based on the racial and ethnic composition of those areas. This discriminatory practice, called redlining, has located many people of color in neighborhoods close to heavy industry and has limited or excluded investment in nearby parks and greenspaces. The Parramore neighborhood of Orlando, Florida, is a living example. Parramore was growing, with successful businesses and relatively good economic development until city planners crafted public policy that disadvantaged folks of color. Housing projects were built, moving poor black families in and white families out. And an interstate was built—a symbol of class and racial divide—displacing Parramore homes and businesses and splitting Parramore from downtown Orlando. Entirely encircled by highways, many serious health consequences have been tied to the pollution and noise that inevitably comes from living there—conditions contributing to a generalized state of overwhelm.

In an article entitled "Even Breathing Is a Risk in One of Orlando's Poorest Neighborhoods," Julia Craven describes the deteriorating conditions in Griffin Park, a federal housing project in Parramore. "The pollution in Griffin Park and its low-income Parramore neighborhood is violence of a kind Americans tend to ignore. But it is as deliberate and as politically determined as any more recognizable act of racial violence. What happened to Griffin Park was the sum of a series of choices made over the course of a century, the effect of which was to transmute formal segregation into the very air certain people breathe." She goes on to assert, "Segregation persists, entrenched through housing and zoning policy and through the construction of urban expressways that literally turned existing racial borders to concrete. This was not an unintended consequence; this was the whole point."

Communities that once thrived are now faced with managing growing homelessness, decaying school systems, and an ever-increasing opioid crisis. Gentrification is displacing once-established low-income, minority residents in urban areas. And in other places, lack of effective public policy in response to factory and mine closures and farm consolidations have left small towns and rural communities in decline. Those left behind or pushed out are struggling to make ends meet, which, as we've seen around the world, can contribute to a rise in generalized anxiety, depression, and anger. During an interview with organizer and activist DeRay Mckesson, Kentucky Congressman John Yarmuth said, "The most important issue in Kentucky is the opioid crisis. In my district it's the number one cause of death right now. We're losing in my district a person a day to overdoses. It's just a horrible situation. One statistic that came out the other day was that in my district alone over the last four and a half years there have been 197 million doses of prescription painkillers prescribed—which is like 250 for every man, woman, and child in the district."

Immigrants, refugees, and anyone deemed "other" are often exposed to conditions that breed overwhelm as fear and rage are displaced onto them in country after country. This, of course, adds to an already heart-breaking cycle, where people who have fled unrest and violence in their country of origin become the target of further persecution in places they were told, or had hoped, they'd find respite.

Another place I have seen communities truly despair is living in the aftermath of violence, whether it be the accumulation of individual acts or a larger-scale attack. While the news cycle moves on and routines resume the veneer of normality, it's critical to remember that the legacy of collective overwhelm usually outlasts the collective stamina to pay attention or redress harm. When I sat with a group of teachers and administrators a couple of years after the massacre that devastated their school, one teacher said, in an anguished voice, "Those six minutes continue to take so much from us."

TWO

What Causes Overwhelm?

The litany of factors contributing to our sense of overwhelm is long. We'll uncover some of the contributors here, but the point is this: The conditions for overwhelm exist for every one of us, whether we were born into them, walk consciously into them, or they descend upon us. But being aware of the many directions from which waves of overwhelm may come can help prepare us to navigate those waves with more self-compassion and prowess. And if we are lucky . . . grace.

"It's a new anti-depressant—instead of swallowing it, you throw it at anyone who appears to be having a good time."

I don't think we can have too much humility and compassion toward ourselves and others as we consider what may cause overwhelm. I learn over and over through my work with trauma survivors just how deeply personal and subjective our experiences are about everything from feeling maxed out to actually being traumatized. Psychiatrist Dr. Mark Epstein reminds us that, "Trauma is not just the result of major disasters. It does not happen to only some people. An undercurrent of trauma runs through ordinary life, shot through as it is with the poignancy of impermanence."

External and internal forces

Epigenetics

The emerging science of epigenetics is based on the theory that environmental factors—from plagues or pollution to deprivation through starvation or war—could affect not just an individual's current physical state but the DNA of subsequent generations as well, including their proclivity to experience overwhelm. According to Professor Marcus Pembrey, a geneticist at University College London and the University of Bristol, "epigenetics is a change in our genetic activity without changing our genetic code."

There is plenty of research to back up the notion that chronic stress in childhood can have long-term impact and alter our genes. Joan Kaufman, director of the Child and Adolescent Research and Education program at the Yale School of Medicine, analyzed DNA in the saliva of children who had been removed from parents due to abuse or neglect and children in a control group. Children who had experienced adversity in early childhood showed epigenetic differences in almost 3,000 sites on their DNA as well as on all twenty-three chromosomes. Scientists attribute the changes to the constant stream of fight-or-flight hormones that kids in crisis experience, impairing their ability to respond to stress. Seth Pollak, professor of psychology and director of the Child Emotion Research Laboratory at the University of Wisconsin, narrowed this down further, identifying that trauma, abuse, or neglect can damage the gene responsible for calming one's internal alarm system in times of stress. "A crucial set of brakes are off," says Pollak.

Epigeneticists also believe that environmental conditions or traumatic experiences leave markers on our DNA that could get passed on to offspring, so someone could exhibit genetic patterns of having been exposed to extreme stress or trauma without having been originally exposed themselves. Dr. Rachel Yehuda, director of Mount Sinai's Traumatic Stress Studies Division, says, "Epigenetic changes often serve to prepare offspring for an environment similar to that of the parents." Her team's study examining Holocaust survivors and their children revealed that survivors have lower levels of the hormones necessary to help the body return to normal after trauma than non-Holocaust survivors. But their descendants *also* have lower levels than normal, which could predispose them to anxiety disorders. Similar effects have been found studying survivors of famine and the September 11 attacks and their descendants.

On the flip side, Barbara Fredrickson, a psychologist from the University of North Carolina at Chapel Hill, posed the next logical question: "If stressful states, including loneliness, caused the genome to respond in a damaging way, might sustained positive experiences have the opposite result?" Together with professor of medicine Steve Cole at UCLA, Dr. Fredrickson has conducted multiple studies on humans regarding the effect of eudaimonic happiness on individuals' physical health. (What is eudaimonic happiness? Aristotle describes it as not just a feeling, but a practice—happiness driven by a sense of meaning, or purpose.) Fredrickson believes that a key facet of eudaimonia is *connection*. "It refers to those aspects of well-being that transcend immediate self-gratification and connect people to something larger."

Data from Fredrickson and Cole's studies demonstrate that our eudaimonic happiness does translate to quantifiable mental and physical well-being at a genetic level. According to Cole, "Those with high levels of eudaimonic happiness had the opposite gene profile of those who experience social isolation: Their antiviral response was up, and their inflammation levels were down." In effect, according to Cole, the stress reaction requires "mortgaging our long-term health in favor of our short-term survival." If we are overwhelmed and lacking eudaimonic happiness, our genetic makeup reflects it. However, how much we pass this on to our descendants is yet to be determined.

Intergenerational oppression and trauma

Intergenerational oppression and trauma is the transmission of the legacies of colonization, marginalization, and historical trauma across multiple generations. Pain is often directly transferred—adult to child—through unconscious anxiety, PTSD, self-medicating and substance abuse, undermined parenting practices, behavioral challenges, and violence.

"That's the racist bone in your body you claimed you didn't have."

As discussed earlier, the scientific evidence that this trauma is heritable through epigenetic changes is growing. But as often happens with scientific discovery, the emerging insights of epigenetics echo experiential evidence about intergenerational trauma shared within communities for generations. As educator and research fellow Shea Robison points out, in Native American culture it's been long-understood that experiences are imprinted and passed down generation to generation.

For example, the group of Lakota Sioux youth who started the camp at Standing Rock in 2016 to protest the Dakota Access Pipeline was initially formed to address a wave of teenage suicides in their tribe. The teens trace a history of poverty, violence, and drug abuse to the hopelessness that pervades their community and has for generations. "No one realizes what the repercussions of colonization have been, the repercussions of forced removal," youth activist Eryn Wise said. "The abuse lives in our blood," said Jasilyn Charger, a founding member of the youth group now called the One Mind Youth Movement. They are trying to overcome that trauma by turning towards their futures and the future of their nation. Charger explained their philosophy: "Forgive, and then take action to spare those who are coming in the future. We don't want our children to inherit this depression."

While some groups are managing the long-term effects of trauma and oppression, for others the problems are just beginning. In January 2017, the University of Michigan released a study showing that the trauma associated with anti-immigration scapegoating can be passed to infants, stating "Babies born to Latina mothers within 37 weeks of [an] immigration raid in Iowa had a 24% greater risk of low birth weight and an increased risk of preterm birth." And it's no surprise that mental trauma affects large numbers of refugees worldwide. The long-term effects on descendants is yet to be determined, but social stigma associated with mental health within the refugee community, combined with a scarcity of mental health specialists for those seeking support, continue to present significant barriers to tending to overwhelm.

Systematic oppression and internalized oppression

When oppression is codified into law or integrated into the functioning of social systems—based on a widespread belief that a certain group of people are inferior—this becomes systematic oppression. Internalized oppression sets in when the people targeted by oppression come to believe the misinformation used to dehumanize them. We witness this bias both in fleeting interactions throughout our days and in persistent, heartbreaking harms that plague our societies.

Processing momentary, yet constant, exertions of oppressive power takes its toll. I know for me, watching prejudice and oppression play out in the lives of young people can be particularly disheartening.

During a family trip, we found ourselves out in the ocean with two boys who couldn't have been older than seven or eight. We didn't pay much attention to the snippets of banter we caught over the surf until we heard one boy encourage the other to try to catch one of the upcoming waves. His buddy replied, exasperated, "These are *lady* waves!" in an eerie singsong voice, with taunting emphasis on l-a-d-y.

I know an acupuncturist who has never *not* been double screened by TSA in U.S. airports since 2001. Every single time he's flown, he has been pulled aside, interrogated, and rescreened. And just the other day, during a visit to a post office in what some would classify as "the hood" in a large U.S. city, I looked up when I heard a white postal worker say to her black coworker in a hushed tone, "Don't ever hand scissors over the counter to a customer." That, in and of itself, didn't seem too disconcerting. But then, in an even more hushed tone, she said, "Particularly in *this* post office." I felt my stomach turn. Her coworker graciously replied, "Oh, okay, sorry. There are so many rules . . ." Her colleague resumed speaking and said, "I know. Each post office is supposed to have the same rules, but we follow our own."

When working at a university that had, amid major conflict, changed its logo from a racist one to a nonracist one, I had the opportunity to spend time with students who are a part of an ever-growing Native American program at the school. In addition to all the structural forces they had to endure as the legacy of colonization continues to unfold, they talked about how painful it was during homecoming weekend to have so many of the older alum insist on wearing their gear from before the mascot had changed, just because they felt "nostalgic."

These fleeting expressions of oppressive power are daunting enough, but they don't operate in a vacuum. They are located in the larger structures that shape our institutions and relationships at the systems level. An instructive example of systematic oppression is how it manifests within the U.S. prison industrial complex and prisons, jails, and detention facilities around the world. In a 2016 report by Penal Reform International, the foreword begins by reminding us, "The human rights of prisoners are a topic that typically elicits limited public attention and even less public sympathy. But it is behind the walls of prisons, police cells and other places of detention that international commitments by Governments to respect, protect and fulfil human rights are perhaps most regularly put to the test."

The U.S. has the highest incarceration rate in the world, and the criminal justice system is defined by stark racial disparities. Where I live and in communities all over the United States, coalitions are trying to address the school-to-prison pipeline trend. According to the ACLU, "children are funneled out of public schools and into the juvenile and criminal justice systems. Many of these children have learning disabilities or histories of poverty, abuse, or neglect, and would benefit from additional educational and counseling services. Instead, they are isolated, punished and pushed out . . . Students of color are especially vulnerable to push-out trends and the discriminatory application of discipline."

It is widely known that folks of color are overrepresented in the system and suffer greatly from a disproportionate denial of liberty. If current trends continue, one in three African American males and one in six Latino males will be incarcerated in their lifetime. According to The Sentencing Project, American Indian youth are three times as likely as white youth to be held in a juvenile detention facility. Research shows that the path to prison often begins in schools and the foster care system: 68 percent of all males in state and federal prison do not have a high school diploma, and 70 percent of California state prison inmates are former foster care youth. And having spent time working in a women's correctional facility, I saw a small window into the disturbing data by The Institute for Criminal Policy Research showing that the number of women and girls in prison "has increased by about 50 percent since the year 2000, a period in which the general world population rose by just 18 percent." With women, too, racial disparity continues to follow a deeply unnerving trendline.

While media (music, television, or film) can either exacerbate oppression or deeply transform it, we're seeing a growing platform of media outlets challenging stereotypes and promoting equality. I appreciated hearing actress Dawn-Lyen Gardner talk about her experience on the show *Queen Sugar*. She discussed fostering activism within her art, sorting through the oppression and internalized oppression she's grown up with and processing the healing that has happened while working with two of her idols, producer Oprah Winfrey and director Ava DuVernay. "Walking as a black woman in this world . . . there is such pressure for perfection, and there is such pressure to stand strong and hold up the world. Even if it's your private world. You gotta be able to hold it up. I think that we are in conversations, especially in television, about all the different ways that we look and feel and those ways including vulnerability and those ways including imperfection and those ways including flaws."

While it's possible for individuals to do the work to metabolize the effects of bias and oppression against them, it is absolutely critical that we own our part in dismantling systematic oppression every day— whenever we can and however we can.

"No, we're good. This gentleman accidentally touched my breast and I accidentally broke his nose."

Health

Our health fluctuates throughout our lifetime, and while there are some who are effortlessly healthful and astonishing in both the quality and longevity of their lives, there are others whose entire lives are consumed by chronic health challenges and brutal conditions within—whether physiological, mental health-related, or both. Many find themselves residing somewhere between those two ends of the continuum, whether they are managing prediabetes indicators or navigating aging. But any health concern has the potential to elicit feelings of overwhelm.

"Your x-rays are kind of depressing so here's me and Susan in front of the Eiffel Tower."

While some elements of our health are outside of our individual control, some may be within our control. Here again we must consider our questions on conditions: How am I contributing? Do I understand the toll? Am I mitigating or exacerbating?

An essential element of our health is related to sleep. A poll by the National Sleep Foundation found that pain, stress, and poor health are key factors contributing to reduced sleep duration and poor sleep quality. But those are not the only stressors on our sleep. Too many of us are still intentionally skimping on sleep. Even though some of us can remember being trained in a bedtime routine as children—transitioning from stimulating to calming activities; turning on sleep signals by following the rituals of quieting down, brushing our teeth, and washing up; changing into pjs; and reading a bedtime story before turning off the lights—more and more people have abandoned the wisdom of this early training. We are suffering the consequences.

Matthew Walker, director of the Center for Human Sleep Science at the University of California, Berkeley, shares, "I think one of the problems with insufficient sleep is people are not very good at predicting how poorly they are doing when they are underslept. So, your subjective sense of how well you're doing is a miserable predictor of, objectively, how you're doing. It's a little bit like the drunk driver at a bar. They've had a couple of shots and some beer, and they stand up, and they say, 'Well, I'm perfectly fine to drive home.' And you say, 'No, I know that you think you're fine to drive, but trust me. Objectively, you're not.' And the same is true for sleep. So, I think many people walk through their lives in an underslept state, not realizing it. It's become this new natural base line." I know a pediatrician who urges parents and guardians to not allow their children to get behind a wheel if they've had fewer than six hours of sleep. She absolutely considers it driving while impaired.

Sleep allows us to consolidate memories and transfer all the bits and pieces of information and experience that we acquire from short-term memory to long-term memory. Without sleep, we significantly decrease our ability to retain information and memories, leading to increased susceptibility to feeling overwhelmed.

Fortunately, there may be a movement to educate folks on the importance of sleep and collectively change our sleep culture. Dr. Matthew Carter, a Williams College professor, shared with me, "I see sleep deprived students all the time, especially in the latter half of each semester. During the last two weeks of the semester, you can't walk through the library without seeing some students asleep at their desks and chairs. Even more alarming, students seem to really mark sleep deprivation as a badge of honor. They know it is very uncomfortable to be sleep deprived, but if they are busy enough to need to stay awake into the night, they think they are very hard workers who are trying their best." In response, Carter is developing curriculum for a new class to help students better understand the critical role sleep plays in their lives. He said, "I'm going to try *my* best to counter that with a campaign I'm creating to help link the importance of sleep with the quality of productivity!"

Eric Fanning, former secretary of the army, points to a shift in the military, too. "Sleeping used to be seen as a weakness in the military. You know, commanders wouldn't sleep when their soldiers were on patrol. Now we realize that sleep deprivation weakens you, and now we teach it as a pillar of strength: Sleep."

As a concept, the critical nature of adequate sleep may be still gaining traction, but the value of good food is not a source of dispute. Despite all the nutritional resources available, an endless stream of wellness marketing campaigns, and the fact that so many folks *talk* about their food programs or dieting strategies *all the time,* on balance we still eat poorly, as confirmed by The Center for Science in the Public Interest, which reports: "Four of the top 10 leading causes of death in the U.S. are directly influenced by diet: Heart disease, cancer, stroke, and diabetes."

Making better food choices is possible. Being mindful about portion sizes and consuming less food is possible. But the dominant culture is not supporting or promoting such choices. The lack of continuous consciousness around food contributes to a constant state of overwhelm. Actor and filmmaker Tom Hanks, when describing being told that he could control his type 2 diabetes after a new diagnosis, conceded, "[it's] the horrifying and dangerous conceit of putting my fate in my own hands. Which means I'm going to just have to pony up and start taking it seriously."

So why do we make poor choices? David Kessler, former commissioner of the Food and Drug Administration, points to the high quantity of fats, sugars, and salts added to processed foods to boost flavor and extend their shelf life. Here's how we fall into an unhealthy cycle: When we are stressed or anxious, fatty, sugary junk food satisfies the reward center of our brains (signaling pleasurable emotions). Sleep deprivation causes those reward centers to be more active (craving more pleasure) while simultaneously suppressing our executive function, effectively diminishing our willpower. And the more junk food we eat, the more chemically dependent we become on the junk food high.

Also, junk food tends to be the most convenient and inexpensive food to purchase and consume quickly. After all, not everyone has access to affordable fruits, vegetables, whole grains, and other foods that may make up a nutritious diet. Many Americans live in food deserts—lacking easy access to grocery stores with fresh, nourishing options—and they are forced to rely on meals from fast food restaurants or corner convenience stores.

In places like Detroit, where more than half of the residents were said to live in a food desert just a decade ago, people are looking for solutions to develop more self-reliant communities and strengthen their local food system. Neighbors in the North End neighborhood of Detroit, for example, are testing a co-op model—partnering with local farms to source food while giving neighborhood residents a chance to have more control over their food choices and increase ownership in their community. This is part of the growing food justice movement, inspiring communities to "exercise their right to grow, sell, and eat food that's fresh, nutritious, affordable, culturally appropriate, and grown locally with care for the well-being of the land, workers, and animals." But food justice must also address the *time* to cook and eat and clean up after wholesome meals.

"We couldn't find a raw-vegan, gluten-free, sugar-free, non-G.M.O. cake for your birthday, so we got you nothing."

In many households, there is no bandwidth for creating and sustaining a healthful food culture, because of changes in family structures or because adults are working multiple jobs to make ends meet. In the U.S., more people are working more hours to make the same wages as before, and the economic imperative that we consume more and buy and take care of more stuff, and all the tech gadgetry and time sucks with social media and more . . . there is simply much less time for people to do things like slow cook food. We don't even *eat* slowly. A fifth grader shared with me that in her school students are given only twenty-five minutes to eat lunch. Twenty-five minutes to leave class, go to their locker, drop off their books, wait in line, get their food, eat their food, get their books, and make it to their next class. Adults are rushed, too. More and more of us are eating on the run. In Seattle, eating-while-driving became enough of a problem to influence a law passed to try to curb the growing number of distracted drivers.

One can be inspired by nations from Spain to Guatemala that have maintained a strong cooking and familial eating tradition. In these cultures, an integrated and grounded view on food isn't just about nutrition, it's also about the entire cycle of preparing, sharing, and concluding a meal. The meal and time relaxing together is so ubiquitous that it's built into the fabric of the entire culture. It can be a place for gratitude for the natural world and for the people who grew the food and prepared the food—as well as a custom for enjoying the food in communion together.

It's also important to acknowledge the potential impact that the advent of screen time and social media may have on our mental health. Psychologist Dr. Jean Twenge, in an article titled "Have Smartphones Destroyed a Generation?" dubs the generation born between 1995 and 2012, shaped by the rise of the smartphone and social media, as iGen. She writes: "The arrival of the smartphone has radically changed every aspect of teenagers' lives, from the nature of their social interactions to their mental health. These changes have affected young people in every corner of the nation and in every type of household. The trends appear among teens poor and rich; of every ethnic background; in cities, suburbs, and small towns. Where there are cell towers, there are teens living their lives on their smartphone." Twenge goes on to explain, "It's not an exaggeration to describe iGen as being on the brink of the worst mental-health crisis in decades. . . . The twin rise of the smartphone and social media has caused an earthquake of a magnitude we've not seen in a very long time, if ever. . . . The number of teens who feel left out has reached all-time highs across age groups. Like the increase in loneliness, the upswing in feeling left out has been swift and significant."

Speaking of loneliness, adults may also be facing what researchers are calling a "loneliness epidemic." After studying the effects of social connection on health around the world, Julianne Holt-Lunstad, professor of psychology at Brigham Young University, said, "There is robust evidence that social isolation and loneliness significantly increase risk for premature mortality, and the magnitude of the risk exceeds that of many leading health indicators."

Our commitments

Family and community

One's family or community of origin and early upbringing provides an incredible foundation for some people, and their familial connection remains a source of tremendous strength. For others, not so much. And for many, our families and community provide a complex combination of both: some gifts and some heartbreak.

"We're going to see my family. There's an extra twenty in it for you if we never get there."

We may get stuck in patterns within our families of origin that we continue to play out as adults, even when the pattern no longer serves us. For example, due to familial circumstances, a child may assume a role as a caretaker, rescuer, victim, or scapegoat. As we mature, those roles may feel unnatural, or even unbearable, and become a source of overwhelm. But, again, we need to objectively ask ourselves: Is this helpful? Is this harmful? If it's not edifying, in order to sustain, we need to take action to relieve the tension and deconstruct those patterns.

Of course, we are all the product of the best *and* the worst of our upbringing. It's the integration of the two that informs so many of our own strengths and weaknesses. The yin and yang of light and shadow—in our families and our communities of origin—shape us. As one colleague, exposed to horror in his youth, said to me, "For me, the baseline is: Life is bad, and then there are these moments of good. I saw my first public execution at age four, so that's my baseline."

Besides the imprint of our ancestral history that we carry within us, our own physical well-being, and the decisions we make about nourishing our bodies with adequate sleep and nutrition, circumstances around one's current family, friends, and community often include aspects that are in and out of our individual control. One may be blessed with steadfast and consistent relationships throughout our lives, but more often life is punctuated with times of connection and times of alienation. Overwhelm takes hold when our experience of the ebb and flow of coming together and growing apart is eclipsed by regrets and all the ways we feel we're falling short. As Jack Kornfield says, "There's a *reason* they call it a *nuclear* family."

To this day, I feel ashamed at how I handled my partner's recovery after his second (of three) hip replacement surgeries. [Don't ask. His hip got recalled.] My entire career has been devoted to trauma, so for me surgeries do not indicate a fresh start. They remind me of every single grieving family member I've ever worked with who has lost a loved one in a hospital. So his first hip replacement was challenging enough, but either I completely repressed it, or I didn't realize how spent I'd been, until his second hip needed replacing. Surgery went well. We brought him home to convalesce. Our children were young, we had a preschool in our home, our house was under construction for the millionth time, and I remained involved in trauma work.

On that morning, I needed to tend to our clamoring children, make sure all was okay at the preschool, host a meeting at our house for my other work, and make sure my partner was okay. [I am not exaggerating when I say he is the best patient, in my experience. So gracious, so thoughtful. Tries to be helpful even when he literally cannot move.] Early that morning, he asked if I could get him some breakfast. "Totally!" I said. Some time went by. He asked again. "Absolutely!" I said. Then I heard the front door bell ring. I suddenly realized what time it was and that I had to answer the door and get my partner fed. I ran to the kitchen, my eyes landed on a bunch of bananas on the counter, I grabbed them and ran to his convalescing room, and I chucked the bananas across the room. They spiraled through the air and landed on his chest as the door closed. There is no—zero, absolutely not *one*—excuse I could make for that moment. Ever. And while it's one of his favorite stories to tell— laughing each time he recounts it—I didn't entirely realize how much I'd messed up until a couple of years later while we were preparing the same room for his *third* hip surgery. Once everything was in place for his return home, he left the room, went to the kitchen, got a full box of Clif Bars, and placed them securely on the table right next to the bed.

While it doesn't make me feel better about my shortcomings, I am not alone in feeling the disconnect between how we hope we can show up in our relationships and the reality. A colleague of mine took time away from a career that she was deeply dedicated to in order to be at home full- time, caring for her baby. She once said to me in a moment where despair was creeping in, "I don't think parenting is using my best skill set."

The weight of trying to do right in our relationships can be felt in our day-to-day dealings with family and loved ones, to say nothing of when we lose someone we love. I knew a grieving father who had lost his fifteen-year-old son suddenly. He received an outpouring of support from the community. But the one request he made, which I will always remember, was for his son's friends and classmates to come over after school and on the weekends just to do their homework in the kitchen where his son used to do his.

The effects of being overwhelmed are most often not linear, and this can add to the challenges that accompany being overwhelmed in the first place. My daughter experienced five suicides within a twelve-month period. After losing a beloved classmate to suicide in her first year of high school, she grieved throughout the year, with feelings that were more intense sometimes than others, and was acutely aware when the anniversary of her classmate's death was approaching. She tended to it in all the ways she knew how, but nothing could prepare her for the wave of grief that crashed over her midway through a basketball game on the day of his yahrzeit. She managed to (barely) get through the game, but once off the court, trying to hold back tears, she described being completely and totally disoriented. She couldn't see properly, couldn't hear well, and her behavior almost paralleled that of someone with a severe concussion. Grief, like a series of waves, is not in our individual control. It doesn't typically follow a pattern or crescendo or decrescendo in equal measure. Big waves may be followed by a series of smaller waves, but the rogue waves are still out there. Never turn your back on the ocean.

School

School in our youth or later in life—while a privilege when we have the opportunity—can be a breeding ground for competition, intimidation, harassment, and discrimination. A recipe for overwhelm.

"We've unleashed your child's potential—this is as good as it's going to get."

While a scholastic environment can be hard to navigate at any stage, in the U.S. we have seen the pressure once reserved for elite, higher ed institutions seeping into grades as early as middle school. Between the complex social landscape (navigating cohort dysfunction, hookup culture, and drugs and alcohol) and academic pressures, person after person I spoke with had a physical response when talking about their school-related stress levels. Stress stems from both being at school *and* the whole social media world surrounding school. My youngest daughter and I were in the car a few days after her seventh-grade year ended, while the decompression was still slowly taking place. There was a long pause in our conversation, then she said in a soft, slow voice, "I think back on this year and just feel so, so bad for my stressed-out self."

The pressures aren't exclusive to the U.S., though. During a family trip to Ecuador, we had the privilege of visiting a school on a remote island. Our fifteen-year-old guide was telling us all about herself and described an exam she had been studying for. My daughters nodded their heads, agreeing, totally in sync: Yes, exams are hard, exams are stressful, totally, right on. Then, as our guide slowly started describing what was hinging on the results from this exam, my daughters' heads stopped nodding, their eyes got bigger, they each became slightly slack jawed. In six months, she would take an exam that would determine what options she would have for school—thus her profession, thus her livelihood for the rest of her life—if she chose to stay in Ecuador. I could tell from the looks in my girls' eyes that they knew then that they would never, ever experience school pressure as weighty, and potentially as crushing, as that.

Some schools are trying to interrupt forces contributing to students' overwhelm by reminding students that there's no such thing as perfection and that making mistakes can be a sign of courage, growth, and creativity. One of our family friends sat with 1,100 of his fellow first-year college students at a gathering only hours after they'd moved into their dorms. The president of the university, a former NASA rocket scientist, encouraged them to look around and appreciate their new peers. She cautioned the students that even though a large swath of them had earned 4.0s in high school (many were valedictorians of their class) that every one of them would make mistakes during the upcoming year. In fact, they should all *expect to fail* at something. But, she reassured them, failure is not to be feared. Failing can foster fortitude.

Work

In the aggregate, we hope to find enjoyment and a sense of purpose in our work that is not eclipsed by overwhelm for more than a bearable stretch at a time. However, work can be extremely difficult. One's work varies from jobs to careers, and challenges can range from just being able to find viable work in the first place, to wading through dynamics with one's coworkers and colleagues, to facing outright discrimination and harassment all the way through inadequate restroom facilities. As one colleague said to me, "The work itself is the least of my concerns. It's all of my pain-in-the-ass coworkers that are the real problem." I took pause as to just how extreme folks' work environments can be when a colleague at a residential youth center said, "I served three tours in combat zones and was in the military for twenty-eight years. That was a breeze compared to what we've got going on here."

It is worth noting that while there are the jobs and professions that require indisputably brutal work, we never want to compare hardship or suffering. And it is not only trauma-filled work that can create conditions of overwhelm—many fields and circumstances may contribute to content or an environment that is overwhelming. President of HBO Documentary Films Sheila Nevins shared in an interview, "I mean, I think if you're a surgeon, the person is anesthetized when you're cutting out their heart. But when you're making a documentary the person [you are focused on] is alive and kicking and they stay with you. You see sadness all the time. There is a lot of suffering in this world. There are a lot of people who have no way out. Without empathy there's no humanity. It stays with you. It's very difficult. I mean you really agonize. I agonize."

Many folks are just plain overworked. The European Union mandates a minimum of twenty days of paid vacation per year (exclusive of bank holidays), and many countries, including Sweden, France, and Denmark, allocate even more. The U.S., however, has no federal laws guaranteeing paid time off for workers, or even breaks for national holidays.

Sadly, more than half of U.S. workers with paid leave don't take all their paid time off, and those who do often obsessively check and respond to emails while out of the office. Research reveals the biggest barriers to taking vacation: fears that employees would return to a mountain of work (37 percent) and a belief that no one else can do the job (30 percent). And six in ten employees report a lack of support for taking time off from their boss. As one partner at a law firm said to me, "In my professional and social culture there is an unconscious message that if you aren't overwhelmed ['How have you been?' 'Sooo freaking busy.' 'Me too!'] you are not measuring up."

"Everybody's getting together after work to do some more work—you in?"

Being overwhelmed in a professional context has been proven to decrease productivity and happiness no matter the profession and no matter where you live. In fact, information overload itself is a growing problem. We are overwhelmed by the sheer volume of information we are expected to sift through, decipher, and categorize. As writer Colleen Story put it, "Pretty soon you end up with a congested brain. If it had nostrils, it wouldn't be able to breathe." According to an international poll commissioned by LexisNexis, 51 percent of almost 2,000 white collar professionals across the U.S., Europe, Asia Pacific, and Africa reported that if the amount of information they receive in their chosen profession continues to increase, they will reach "a breaking point." One colleague shared, "I feel sunburned on the inside."

Many professionals have shared with me that the stress of work is not just contained to the work day. By any stretch. Through laptops or phones, they are bombarded with work from early in the morning to late at night through texts, notifications, and conference calls at all hours. There can also be an anticipatory dread that seeps in for folks on Sundays (for those who work Monday through Friday) or days before a project begins. This is similar to the students I know (ranging from middle school through graduate school) who dread Sundays—*almost* as much as they dread the beginning of the school year. One child abuse prevention specialist described his angst about how he'd feel leading up to a particular rotation: "I'm generally a glass-is-half-full kind of person. But as impending work challenges loom closer, I don't like how impatient I get. At home. For the week before, too. I start dreading my work days in advance."

Environment

Economic stressors

Stress caused by the economy is well documented and experienced on a global scale. Many economists have noted the dangers of unchecked capitalism, especially in terms of the unyielding drive to greater and greater production and consumption. People across the economic spectrum and around the world are more overwhelmed with less resources where it counts—time for family, education, and community engagement. Professor and author Dr. William Robinson, in his article "The Great Recession of 2008 and The Continuing Crisis: A Global Capitalism Perspective," speaks of a crisis of social polarization. "I want to evoke here the concept of global crisis in a broader sense. This crisis, in my view, is unprecedented in terms of its magnitude, its global reach, the extent of ecological degradation and social deterioration, and the scale of the means of violence. Moreover, because the system is now global, crisis in any one place tends to represent crisis for the system as a whole."

Economic stressors, of course, are tied into countless areas of our lives. When asked what he would say to those who are losing hope, who feel like the world is imploding, Kentucky Congressman John Yarmuth said, "I wish I could offer comfort in that regard. I'm not given to exaggeration and hyperbole . . . but I've never been more concerned about the stability of our democracy."

World events

The impact of the 24-hour news cycle on our collective state of overwhelm is notable. What's transpiring in the world, as well as how we're taking it all in, is where I see a lot of folks reach a tipping point. Of course, there are stunning, heroic, generous, grace-filled moments and events every day, everywhere. Also, there is indescribable anguish and horror. Traditional media and social media are bringing these reports and first-hand accounts into our lives in ever-increasing rates. And while some of it we can absolutely do something about, much of it remains outside of our individual control. So, the content, the volume of content, and the omnipresence of delivery systems—whether on massive screens at the gym, on our laptops in the kitchen, on our phones on the bus, in print, or on the radio—can escalate our sense of despair.

All the news and information coming in that is admonishing us to stay "vigilant" is a source of tremendous conflict for many. I cannot count the number of people who have shared with me how desperate they are to consume less media but force themselves to continue to—feeling that if they are not constantly aware of what is happening everywhere, always, then they are not being "good" activists, community members, or citizens. Indeed, the increase in people policing the news feeds of friends and loved ones—to monitor expressions of solidarity, outrage, support, or anxiety over the issues that most concern them—reinforces the worry that taking a break from news is somehow lazy or disloyal.

During a workshop for hospice workers, a hospice nurse shared with her colleagues how she finally had gotten to the point where she couldn't listen to the news anymore, once she realized how much it was affecting her. Like many who work in others' homes, she was in her car hours and hours every day—time she was spending listening to the radio, inundated by a steady stream of breaking world news. I deeply respected this nurse's insight not only into the toll the news was taking on *her* but into how it diminished her ability to show up in the way she needed to for the families she was serving.

"On the plus side, we won't have access to the news for the next four years."

Climate crisis

While not something we have worldwide consensus on, 97 percent of climate scientists agree that human-caused climate change is a reality. While extreme climate-related events used to be described as 1,000-year or 500-year events, many of them are becoming so common that scientists are considering dropping the terminology altogether. According to Dr. Michael Mann, director of the Penn State Earth System Science Center, "we've loaded the dice through climate change so that these events are appearing far more often."

In the context of the effect of climate change on mental health and social activism, Dr. Scott Woodruff, director of the anxiety and obsessive-compulsive treatment program at the American Institute for Cognitive Therapy says, "Excessive worry can lead to fatigue, lack of concentration, and muscle tightness. The fatigue and lack of concentration are the opposite of what people are trying to promote when they're advocating for vigilance."

Over the last few years, I have seen the climate crisis take scientists and other long-term environmental advocates—weathered and experienced individuals, far from being naive—down to their knees with despair. Filmmaker and environmental activist Josh Fox, when talking about how he decided to make the film *Gasland II,* shared, "[We] went down to the Gulf and we managed—I don't know how it happened, whether it was the 4th of July or because it was a Sunday—we got this sort of unprecedented clearance from FAA to fly at any altitude we wanted over the oil spill. And they had previously been restricting flights to 3,000 feet and above and from 3,000 feet you can't see anything . . . When you watch *Gasland II,* you'll see the pictures of the Gulf that you've never seen before. The whole surface for 50 miles streaked with oil . . . I was absolutely dismayed and confused and horrified and in shock. We got off that little airplane and none of us could talk for hours. We were just—we were nonverbal . . . Just seeing the Gulf in that state. Just seeing this entire ocean and the streaks of oil and feeling like a piece of me fell out of the airplane."

I was corresponding with my friend, artist and photographer Chris Jordan the day he returned from the Fourth International Marine Protected Areas Congress in Chile in 2017. He shared, "For me the most amazing thing at the moment is the extent of our denial. Our collective ability to face the realities of our time seems to be moving in the wrong direction in ways that continue to astonish me. I met a biologist from Florida who said that she's not even allowed to use the term 'sea-level rise'; they are all required in Florida to say 'nuisance flooding.' They clench onto this insane narrative despite the obvious incredible irony of it, as the most powerful hurricane in recorded history literally sits over the top of them at this very moment." Chris went on to say, "I guess it is just really hard for us to accept the truth of what we are doing to our world. I think for many people it brings up feelings of hopelessness and impotence on a deep, existential level. We remain locked in collective amygdala hijack right at the crucial moment when we need to be acting decisively. The depth of tragedy that this means for the quality of life of future beings cannot be overemphasized."

"I'm trying to decide between water and sunlight."

One of the things I remind folks in every single field I work in is this: Even if we are not oriented in small or big ways toward climate change in our work or in our lives—as things continue to go the direction they're going—we or our loved ones will most certainly be impacted by climate change, whether we lose access to drinkable water or places to live that are not toxic, or we're pummeled by the increasing ferocity of storms. While floods and fires don't discern where to hit, those who are historically marginalized and historically disenfranchised will be the ones who continue to be disproportionately affected by weather-related destruction. And, for some, that means facing a lifetime of trying to rebuild.

There are so many factors—big and small—contributing to our overwhelm, and still, we can reduce some of the burden simply by acknowledging that most of these factors are not ours alone to resolve and by making space in our lives for that which can sustain us.

THREE

A Way Through:
When Less Is More

As we dive deeper into the art and science of addressing overwhelm—individually and collectively—let's explore *how to metabolize* what we're experiencing and bearing witness to in a constructive and meaningful way, *how and why* we become saturated, and *what to do* about it.

"You should relax less."

We've already discussed many of the factors that can contribute to potential overwhelm. Every single day, we are exposed to countless issues (some beyond our control, some within our control). Some buoy us. Some strengthen us. And some of this exposure can erode us.

When exposure erodes us, we begin to accumulate harm. We accumulate disappointments, slights, and disconnects between what we'd hoped or planned for and reality. We may simply be collecting the weight of lots of small, daily setbacks. (As one of my teachers cautioned me, "Expectations are premeditated disappointments.") Or we may be constantly pummeled with trauma of glacial proportions. But if for any reason we don't tend to this growing accumulation along the way—metabolizing it—we can become saturated.

Our goal, of course, is to focus on doing *less* of that which erodes us and *more* of that which sustains us.

Metabolizing exposure

It's important to manage our exposure levels (whether in our control or not) along with our reaction to it (our ability to metabolize, integrate, and make meaning of it). This can be the proverbial razor's edge: dancing the sharp line created by what we are facing externally; our internal capacity to process it; and our resulting speech, conduct, and action. But here's what I know for certain: When we don't fully metabolize that which may accumulate within us, it tends to linger and fester and then manifest—sometimes horribly; so we must focus on what we *do* have power over, even if it's only our own mind.

Metabolism is made up of two processes: catabolism and anabolism. Catabolism is the breaking apart/breaking down phase, often with the release of molecular energy. Anabolism is the "building up" of necessary nutrients for repair or growth. We break down accrued physical and emotional impact of exposure that erodes us, and we build muscles of capacity to strengthen us. We are aiming for an integrated sense of self, a regulated nervous system, an ever-present internal flow. Equilibrium and homeostasis. Aspiring to experience more times throughout our day when we are able to feel spacious and be in tune with ourselves and our surroundings, because we have metabolized—or processed—our experience.

Relieving saturation

When, however, outside circumstances dominate our internal ability to metabolize all that we are exposed to, we can become saturated. Physiologically. In our nervous system. Saturated. To move forward, maintaining balance, we must constantly be aware of how much we're contending with externally—and, on any given day (or hour), what our internal capacity is to metabolize so that we are saturated as infrequently as possible. What has become ingrained in me—from my own experience and that of my colleagues, from the studying I've done, and from the time I've spent with wise teachers from anti-Apartheid leader Archbishop Desmond Tutu to Thich Nhat Hanh—is that monitoring our exposure and taking measures to help metabolize our experiences is most effective when tended to daily (or daily-ish).

> "Having a tragic view of life is compatible with having a positive view of our worldly duties. This is a big and abstract thought . . . and perhaps, like so many like it, it is teachable only as a pained—at this moment, acutely pained—daily practice."
>
> —Adam Gopnik, journalist and author

Our daily practice may continuously oscillate between "handling your business," as musician and social justice activist Stevie Wonder says, and doing what needs to be done in your life and out in the world. We can get into a rhythm: internal and external, back and forth. Quiet the mind, tend to the world. Former abbot of the Daitoku-ji, Oda Sessō, says, "In Zen, there are only two things, you sit and you sweep the garden. It doesn't matter how big the garden is." Of course, this does not require an actual sitting, but the inestimable value of having a regular, dedicated, contemplative practice—both so we can refrain from causing harm and so we can bring our most impeccable selves early and often—cannot be underestimated.

Part of the reason adopting a daily practice to manage our exposure is important is because we don't do well being saturated. Our fight-flight-freeze response is something we're meant to call on in rare and brief episodes when facing imminent threat. This activated state was never designed to fuel our day-to-day routine; it was not intended as a constant companion.

Being saturated is unpleasant, often perilous, and at times dangerous—so humans don't generally stay saturated for long; there is a hemorrhaging out that happens. This can be an individual hemorrhaging or a collective hemorrhaging. Often there is toxicity in the hemorrhaging. Sometimes it's an isolated act, sometimes it's a pattern of behavior, sometimes it's the palpably foul feeling within a school or agency or community. These days, entire families are saturated, schools are hemorrhaging out, organizations are saturated, businesses are hemorrhaging out. And in our hemorrhaging, we do damage to ourselves, our loved ones, those folks we cut off in traffic, our coworkers we talk over in meetings, those we bully online or in person, and *much*, much worse. In a best-case scenario, collateral consequences can be cleaned up with a sincere apology. Frequently, however, the harm we cause may be permanent, or even wide-scale and reprehensible.

It is worth noting that hemorrhaging is not a reference to the intentional and deliberate release of current accumulation—or a backlog of accumulation—individually or collectively. When I speak of hemorrhaging, I'm not talking about sweating while you lift weights, having a friend listen as you rant (with their permission), allowing tears to stream down your face, or lying on the ground having a grown-up tantrum. Nor is it attending a community-wide vigil, showing up at a peaceful protest, or participating in a campus-wide stress-releasing scream at a designated hour. Hemorrhaging is more along the lines of a slow seething or an abrupt eruption. It's not necessarily conscious nor is it constructive. I was working in a community ravaged by the opioid epidemic when one colleague who had been working a punishing schedule beautifully articulated a consequence of her hemorrhaging out that took her by surprise, sharing, "Even my dog avoids me now."

Acknowledging potential barriers

Finding a way to manage and process your exposure to factors contributing to overwhelm is critical, but let's acknowledge that there may be actual and perceived barriers that arise along the way. We erect a barrier for ourselves when we endorse the notion that being who we are and *not* being overwhelmed are mutually exclusive. We may feel so entrenched in scarcity that we can't wrap our minds around how to do something differently, or we may occupy a place of privilege such that we feel that we, of all people, have an obligation to take on more and more.

And you are not alone if you notice a correlation between trying to do things differently and facing societal headwinds that may add to the degree of difficulty. Even if you are fortunate enough to live in a place cited as leading the world in health, happiness, and work-life balance, there are global forces we may need to contend with.

"Wheatgrass is highly effective at neutralizing joy."

That said, cultures can be found all around the world that are not being enveloped by a state of overwhelm. We are not inventing a fancy new way of *being* here. We must simply remember what is known to us, cherish the wisdom that continues to be passed down from generation to generation, and, hopefully with a solid sense of humor in place, ask ourselves: "Assuming I know what I need to do to handle my business, what are the barriers in my way?" If we are not continuously oriented toward creating that still pond within ourselves from where we can accurately see the reflection of all that is around us, we may benefit from circling back repeatedly to ask ourselves why.

As Jack Kornfield reminds us, "As humans, we are loyal to our suffering." While this shakes out differently for all of us, I think many of us can relate to the tension we feel when we try to make changes in our life. And though tending to this can be daunting, the stakes are too high to ignore.

"I can cure your back problem, but there's a risk that you'll be left with nothing to talk about."

Essential to your ability to mitigate harm is your ability to be with yourself—to have an intrapersonal relationship with oneself. Many of us, for very sound reasons, may lose our ability to tolerate being in our own company for a time, and we need to check out. One contributing factor is our sensitivity to how others perceive us and our investment in our own self-image, which can undermine our ability to fully metabolize experiences and leave us vulnerable to saturation and overwhelm. Of course, the pressures we put on ourselves are inextricably linked to all the messages we get from society at large about the *right* way to grieve, the *expected* way to be a survivor, or the admired way to handle any number of situations in life.

One eighteen-year-old described the pressure she felt the first time she visited the place where her brother had died—a place they had spent their childhoods and a place where they both worked. "I didn't want people to see me cry. I wanted to show them that I am strong and that I can handle things by myself," she explained. "I thought I could gain control of my emotions by bottling them up." Although in the months after his death she spent long days continuing to work at the same site, it was eighteen months later, in the company of only one other person, when she finally allowed herself to feel what she'd been guarding inside; only then did she allow tears to flow freely. Separately, a high school sexual assault survivor conveyed a similar burden to hold it all together. "I don't like people to see me as vulnerable. I want them to see me as strong. Feeling vulnerable reminds me of the assault itself," she shared.

Many of us also place pressure on ourselves daily to strive for perfection. In young and old alike, when we put an impossible degree of pressure on ourselves to perform and get everything right, every time, it can undermine our ability to effectively and meaningfully tend to ourselves. One police officer shared with me, "Look, as police officers, we can't let ourselves be vulnerable. We can't let our loved ones be vulnerable. We can't allow ourselves to be vulnerable because the job is dangerous or because of attacks from the public or because of the legal issues we face or because of the media. So, our inability to be vulnerable means we don't allow ourselves to believe that we need help—of any kind—or that we even could be helped through this." Founder of the Center for Courage & Renewal, Parker Palmer reminds us, "Wholeness does not mean perfection: it means embracing brokenness as an integral part of life."

Cultivating the capacity to accept and be with ourselves—as we are, not how we think we should be—is one of the most important steps we can take toward our ability to sustain in life. In the same week, I heard sixteen-year-olds in a focus group and adult professionals in a staff meeting both say, "I'm generally okay during the day and when I'm distracted, but when I am alone, or at night, that's when the thoughts all rush in and I feel overwhelmed. I can't be by myself." Day or night, whether we are reaching for something to numb us out or occupying our time with distractions, the amount of harm—both individually and collectively—caused by our inability to tolerate being with ourselves is distinctly on the rise.

Feeling the need to escape is not problematic in and of itself if we do it mindfully. I paused for a long moment when I read this in the Apartheid Museum in Johannesburg: "If a man can't drown his troubles away, at least he can make them float for a while." If you need an hour, or a day, to lose yourself in your favorite show, do it deliberately. "Here's me, about to dive into six seasons nonstop. Bring it on, baby!" is quite different than "Whoa! Who knows what happened to my weekend? My device automatically plays episode after episode, and once it's started playing, I don't want to be rude to it and press stop!" So, too, with anything else we lose ourselves in for a time. Pause, notice, and make a deliberate choice instead of unconsciously reaching for a person, a substance, an object, or an activity.

When less is more

While there are absolutely times of true suffering in life when the outside reality is too much for any human to bear for a few minutes, let alone forever—*much* of our individual and collective sense of overwhelm can be addressed readily with subtle shifts of attention, by redirecting our focus without adding countless arduous steps to our already packed to-do list. From a place of self-respect, we should remind ourselves that often the pain, struggle, and hardship we are experiencing are not inevitable. And, then, when those times in our lives do come that may feel too much to bear, then, too, we know we can find a way through. Philosopher Jean-Paul Sartre called genius "not a gift, but the way a person invents in desperate circumstances."

Of course, it goes without saying that we want to be as proactive and preemptive as possible. As a landscaper said sternly to me upon discovering the complete and total neglect of our yard, "If the soil in the area becomes too dry, it becomes hydrophobic and won't take up water easily. Or . . . at all." Let's not let our own selves get to that point.

I remember Tibetan Buddhist nun Pema Chödrön sharing in a dharma talk that whatever we do, that's what we're getting better at. For better or for worse. I have found it helpful to remember this through-out my day, asking: Is this something I want to get better at? *This* might be focusing on everything my family neglected to do around the house, ruminating about a recent political initiative, or stressing about the countless things we all could stress about. And sometimes, when I can remember to tell myself less is more, it cues me to be intentional about what I *do* want to invest in (thought or action-wise) and what is better left alone.

My daughter's friend gave me a gift as it applies to the practice of being conscious about what I want to invest in and when. Picture sixth grade, first school dance of the year . . . somewhat of a surprisingly big deal at this school in terms of what to wear, who to go with, where to get ready, with whom to dance . . . it was a lot. I was the parent scheduled to pick up a group of girls, and as they walked toward me I tried to read each of them to get a sense of how the last three hours had been. They arrived at the car and I asked, "So . . . how was it?" Summariz-ing the experience, this friend said wryly, "I don't think it was worth a dress." We sometimes craft storylines in our imaginations that require so much *more* of us to play out—when *less,* in retrospect, would have been quite enough.

Remember: Even seemingly inconsequential, minute choices can have immeasurable impact. Toward the end of drafting this book, I was waiting alone to eat in a packed restaurant. When offered a table for two, I suggested that the women who were together next in line take the table and I could wait for the next spot available. A few minutes later, still in line, I looked up from my phone when a man stopped in front of me. In a soft voice he said, "That was nice of you, giving up your spot. I just want you to know you restored my faith in humanity today."

When we are not purposeful in circumventing or tending to overwhelm and we become saturated, we increase our susceptibility to compromised states, including (but not limited to) being:

- Distracted
- Disconnected
- Attached
- Depleted

The more saturated we are, the more we fall into these patterns. The more we fall into these patterns, the more saturated we become. But once we identify the patterns, we have an opportunity to address and diffuse them, by adopting constructive practices to metabolize our experiences:

- When we allow ourselves to become distracted → we can focus on being more intentional.
- When we are disconnecting → we can take measures to be more present.
- If we feel ourselves becoming attached, digging in, or becoming entrenched → we can soften this by shifting into a position of curiosity.
- When depleted → we can seek sources to bolster our stamina.

"I had my own blog for a while, but I decided to go back to just pointless, incessant barking."

And here is where the less-is-more approach pays off. Let's focus our attention on doing *less* of that which erodes us and *more* of that which sustains us. You may find, as I have, that focusing on that which is *in our control* serves to lessen the burden of overwhelm, restore our perspective, stabilize us, and give us strength to navigate what is yet to come. The ability to find what works for us, at any given time, remains a constant internal conversation—and the effort required may be small. According to the principle of the "aggregation of marginal gains," if you make a 1 percent margin of improvement in several areas, the cumulative result will be significant gains. As you move through the following chapters, continue to consider: How could you move the needle on managing your overwhelm, 1 percent at a time?

"My 'perfect storm' was nothing permanent. But, of course, it's far from the last storm I'll face. There will be many more. The key is building fires where you can warm yourself as you wait for the tempest to pass. These fires—the routines, habits, relationships, and coping mechanisms you build—help you to look at the rain and see fertilizer instead of a flood."

—Tim Ferriss, author and entrepreneur

FOUR

Less Distraction, More Intention

One evening deep into winter I had a car brimming with swim team kids; it was my turn to drive everyone home. The afternoon was a whirlwind, and nothing had gone as planned. I apologized to the wet swimmers reeking of chlorine and explained that I needed to stop quickly and pick up takeout food. I ran from my car into the restaurant and stopped abruptly at the hostess station. The young woman looked up and asked if she could help me. I told her I had an order that I was very late picking up. She said, "Great, what's your name?" I stood there. She looked at me. I stood there some more. She looked at me. I finally said, "That's a great question." I could not remember my name. As those words left my mouth, one of the women seated at the bar to my right spit out her drink, laughing. My name came back to me, I got my food and turned to leave, feeling very unnerved. The hostess called after me, "Good luck . . . you know . . . with your name and everything!"

We can become so saturated by all that we encounter that we become completely distracted from the very fundamentals. Like, you know, remembering our name.

Additionally, when overwhelm drives our defenses down, we may be drawn to the dopamine rush that comes from many types of distractions. Author and philosopher Aldous Huxley described humans' "almost infinite appetite for distractions" and cautioned, "Used in one way, the press, the radio and the cinema are indispensable to the survival of democracy. Used in another way, they are among the most powerful weapons in the dictator's armory."

Whether, then, it matters to us that we can follow what a friend or family member is saying during a conversation they're attempting to have with us, or whether we are invested in tracking politics and world news, being intentional about *where* we put our focus and *why* is essential to reducing overwhelm. The first step, of course, is acknowledging that which distracts us.

Distracted?

I know this isn't the first place I noticed folks being distracted, but I think because it was so deeply troubling to me, I really took notice of my kids and their friends constantly on their phones. Screen distraction. It seemed like it happened overnight, though, of course, I know that's not true.

To be fair, I, my partner, and so many other adults are awful role models. Awful. Part of my reason for obsessing on it more with the children and teens I spend time with is because we know that screen time is impacting their developing brains differently than it is those of us whose brains are well along on the deterioration road, though excessive screen time is not doing us any favors, either. Distraction via our screens is a prevalent, contemporary concern. While the research continues to come in on all the various effects of screen time—whether video games or social media platforms—on people's brains, most compelling for me has been hearing from a lot of young adults on how they experience it to be such a dominant force in their lives.

Person after person I've interviewed has talked about how they feel the entire social media scene is both out of control in their lives—that it's a "fake world"—yet it's also something they don't feel they have viable options around. "When I tried to get off it, I felt like my relationships were diminishing. There are people I wouldn't go out of my way to text, but if we send each other snaps then we're still friends, right?" Another adolescent said, "Social media is so much of what the teenage world is based in. You're giving up your community once you leave social media. High school is so much about what goes on on our phones." No one I have spoken to defends it, and even while the insight may run deep about all the damaging effects (feeling excluded, status anxiety, what it's like to see curated life after curated life), there is an undercurrent of uncertainty about how to find a way out.

Even the creators of the very technologies that feed our addiction to screens—an addiction reinforced through hits of positive feedback we get from liking or commenting on apps and websites—are trying to disentangle themselves from the mediums. Justin Rosenstein, the Facebook engineer who created the "like" button, describes Facebook likes as "bright dings of pseudo-pleasure that can be as hollow as they are seductive." According to an article in *The Guardian*, Rosenstein now "appears most concerned about the psychological effects on people who, research shows, touch, swipe or tap their phone 2,617 times a day. There is growing concern that as well as addicting users, technology is contributing toward so-called 'continuous partial attention,' severely limiting people's ability to focus, and possibly lowering IQ. One study showed that the mere presence of smartphones damages cognitive capacity—even when the device is turned off. 'Everyone is distracted,' Rosenstein says. 'All of the time.'"

More than one-third of subjects in a study conducted by the University of Cambridge felt overwhelmed by technology and were also more likely to feel less satisfied with their life as a whole. And a study conducted by the University of Maryland showed that a "clear majority" of almost 1,000 university students interviewed in ten countries, including Britain, the U.S., and China, were unable to voluntarily avoid technology for one full day. Students who partook in the study described feelings of intense cravings, anxiety, and depression when they were unable to plug into their phones, the Internet, social media, or television. Twenty percent of participants reported feelings akin to a drug addiction, with little control and immense withdrawal symptoms. Professor Susan Moeller said students "expected the frustration. But they didn't expect to have the psychological effects—to be lonely, to be panicked, the anxiety, literally [experiencing] heart palpitations."

There is distraction via the news and politics. The pull to consistently monitor cable news and news feeds is different than staying informed and different from engaging, resisting, persisting, and contributing wisely. This is another place where so many of us allow ourselves to be distracted in ways that keep us from focusing on both what we have control over and what actually matters. Checking out news feeds that support our ideology (sometimes even unknowingly, given the algorithms choosing for us) and expressing outrage at the latest political twists may provide short-term emotional gratification. But this is not an ideal habit to build. As comedian and television host Stephen Colbert shared, "The pure polarization that is a hit of heroin to those who take pleasure from political strife has no more appeal to me."

"We're close to being reliant solely on renewable sources of outrage."

Writer and educator Clint Smith, when talking about the growing number of people getting their primary news from social media, shared, "I think we can't underestimate the extent to which not only news articles that people are reading shape their ideas about the world but seeing people that they know or follow . . . what *they* have to say about the news . . . how much *that* shapes the way people are thinking about the world."

There is distraction via being caught up in others' business. Many teens get a bad rap for this in terms of creating drama and talking trash, but we adults also have a lot to learn from some of their healthy strategies. Whether when a group of kids overtakes our kitchen or when I'm walking by a high school practice, I have felt heartened hearing how often kids say to each other, sincerely, "You do you." Yet talking about others when they are not present—which frequently devolves into gossiping—continues to be a tempting distraction across the ages. In Judaism it is said that gossiping is talking about anyone's business, positive or negative. To which a friend of mine said, "What do I have left to talk about?"

While social media is certainly not the sole reason we continuously compare what we're *currently doing* to what we *could be doing*, it can certainly exacerbate a perpetual fear of missing out (FOMO). What teens and young adults have shared with me is that one of the most harmful aspects of social media is the unceasing comparing of themselves with others—whether those known to them or those they may never meet. The constant tug of what else is out there can contribute to the difficulty of being in the moment, attentive to what's actually happening in our life or with those with whom we are spending time. As one seventeen-year-old informed me, "Snapchat is more like 'Oh, you weren't invited to that,' but Instagram is 'Oh, I can't afford to do that.'" Benoit Denizet-Lewis shared in an article, "I listened as a college student went on a philosophical rant about his generation's relationship to social media. 'I don't think we realize how much it's affecting our moods and personalities,' he said. 'Social media is a tool, but it's become this thing that we can't live without but that's making us crazy.'"

Social worker Cara Maksimow said it well: "Relationships and friendships have become more superficial with communication being sterile and through social media. Kids with hundreds or even thousands of 'followers' or 'friends' are actually isolated and spend very little time with others, which can create a sense of emptiness that drives more social media activity and it becomes a vicious cycle." I was so impressed when talking with a family friend who had spent a month abroad during his sophomore year of high school. He had been quite homesick at the beginning. Overwhelmed by being so far from home, he had a hard time settling into his new environment. Recognizing the temptation to assuage his discomfort by spending more time on his phone, he very wisely went the other direction by deleting his Snapchat and Instagram apps. Though this confused some of his friends, he explained, "I felt so lonely every time I looked at it. I just had to get rid of it."

As we venture deeper into this conversation, I think it can be helpful to continue to shake off the tendency to assess any of this through a good/bad/right/wrong lens. Instead, we remind ourselves to deepen our awareness of whatever might be at play and ask ourselves: Is this edifying or is this eroding? Is this helpful or is this harmful? For example, being distracted by a strong external focus on others—whether in person or online—can be met with a simple pause, asking ourselves: To what benefit is this? Is obsessively checking my apps to see who's hanging out with whom helping me in any way? Is knowing what this or that celebrity is up to today worth the time spent doing it?

We also see distraction come in terms of ruminating about both the past and future-tripping on what's yet to come. Again, the pressure so many young folks are under in middle school, high school, and college contributes directly to this early programming of anxiety, stemming from either gnashing their teeth over what just went down with a friend, accumulating dread over the next auditions or tryouts, or being consumed by how to make it through high school and what lies after.

This doesn't ease up when we're adults, necessarily. Some of us may have the tendency—or *gift* if you will—of being able to turn the act of planning or preparing for a new experience, event, or trip into a doomsday scenario. (As the hosts of Pod Save America cautiously instruct, we "don't buy green bananas.") I have had so many colleagues tell me over the years, almost word for word, "Even when things seem calm, I'm always waiting for the other shoe to drop." We see folks moving through their days in a permanent state of distraction—anticipating or rehearsing, but not being where they are.

A human's nervous system evolved what neuroscientists call a negativity bias, which throughout our day scans for bad news, and then our brain hones in on whatever feels like a perceived threat. While that process did, and still can, help our immediate survival, it is unhelpful for our overall well-being. We have been conditioned to anticipate trouble. In some cases, impending catastrophe. As one of my teachers reminded us, it has been said: "I have known many sorrows, most of which never happened."

Our split minds keep us from plugging into what's happening as it unfolds by vacillating between memories (the past) and fantasy (the future). We mine the past for what was lost and look for something we can't quite grasp in the future. Alan Watts, author and spiritual teacher, reminds us, "Hurrying and delaying are alike ways of trying to resist the present."

We're also good at distracting ourselves with the accumulation of things. Culture and commerce trick us into thinking we need more . . . better . . . cooler stuff. We get bedazzled by *things*. We should be aware of what we're avoiding by filling virtual shopping carts with abandon. Craving can undermine us.

"To have any particular perception, emotion, memory, or desire, the brain must impose order on chaos, signals on noise . . . this is 'cognitive essentializing.' . . . Naturally, we try to hold onto the ones we like. But since neural processing continually changes, all experiences are fleeting. They slip through your fingers as you reach for them, an unreliable basis for deep and lasting happiness. Yet so close, so tantalizing . . . and so we keep reaching.

> For these reasons, deep down there is a sense of disturbance, not-enoughness, unease. . . . [W]e crave and cling, suffer and harm. As if life were a cup—with a hole in the bottom—that we keep trying to fill."

> —Dr. Rick Hanson

Another pattern we fall into when overwhelmed is distracting ourselves by being steeped in cynicism and criticizing others.

IT STARTS.

"That's what you're wearing?"

We know that cynicism, even cynical humor, has an extremely powerful undercurrent of anger and rage. I was working with a group of medical providers and one doctor commented to her colleagues, "There is so much cynicism in our hospital right now. In our ER, there is a sense many of us have about the patients that all of them are trying to take advantage of us. I understand getting there eventually in your career, but if that is our starting point now . . . ?" and her voice trailed off.

Composer and educator Leonard Bernstein theorized that cynicism is rooted in the fear and anxiety caused by the real possibility that the world could be destroyed at any moment—a possibility unfamiliar to those living before the time of the atomic bomb—and that cynicism restricts our ambition, leading to an unhealthy yearning for instant gratification. As writer and cultural critic Maria Popova explains, "As we grow up and learn to be cynical, we gradually stifle [our] inherent love of learning, turn off our curiosity, and become calcified. Out of that cynicism springs the impulse for instant gratification—the very opposite of the pleasurably protracted challenge of learning."

A friend shared that she once gave a few dollars to a woman who said she needed money for gas. "You know she's getting over on you, right?" said a person walking by. "That lady is here every day hitting people up with that same fake story." "Sure," my friend said, "but do I want to be a person who's suspicious enough that no one can ever get over on me? Or a person who is decent enough to share a few bucks when I can spare it?"

One of the most exhausting parts of balancing between realism and cynicism is scale. When we believe that everybody is simply waiting to get over on us, it can be irresistible to become suspicious of everyone and cynical about everything. Preserving a tender assessment of the human condition, staying curious about why people are doing what they are doing, and not taking other people's failures as personal attacks against ourselves help us resist the allure of cynicism.

I have been intrigued by this intimacy of cynicism, fear, anxiety, and anger for a long time. James Baldwin wrote, "I imagine that one of the reasons people cling to their hates so stubbornly is because they sense, once hate is gone, they will be forced to deal with pain."

It's worth emphasizing the distinction here between *feeling* anger, rage, or cynicism and *acting* on those feelings. The acting piece is where we all get to hold ourselves accountable. I was moved when doctors and nurses from a burn unit disclosed to me their distress about the deeply entrenched cynicism of their team. It had become difficult to continue to provide the high quality of care they'd each aspired to at the start of their career, since the culture on their unit had become one where many shared a belief: "Good people don't get burned."

"Anger is not always, but very often, about status-injury. And status-injury has a narcissistic flavor: rather than focusing on the wrongfulness of the act as such, a focus that might lead to concern for wrongful acts of the same type more generally, the status-angry person focuses obsessively on herself and her standing vis-à-vis others. . . . [W]e are prone to anger to the extent that we feel insecure or lacking control with respect to the aspect of our goals that has been assailed—and to the extent that we expect or desire control. Anger aims at restoring lost control and often achieves at least an illusion of it. To the extent that a culture encourages people to feel vulnerable to affront and down-ranking in a wide variety of situations, it encourages the roots of status-focused anger."

—Martha Nussbaum, philosopher and professor

Practice being intentional

How to tend to our ability to focus—to be intentional about what we attend to, when, and how—has been one of the most important roads through overwhelm for me. Dr. Richard Davidson, founder of the Center for Healthy Minds at the University of Wisconsin, discovered in his research that there are four independent brain circuits that influence our lasting well-being: our ability to maintain positive states or positive emotions, recover from negative states, focus, and be generous. I use this tactically when trying to recalibrate throughout my day. I'll pause briefly and ask myself: So, where am I in terms of being in a positive state or actively regrouping from a not-so-positive state? Where am I putting my focus? And has any part of me—whether in thought or action—been generous today?

John Feal, a first responder at Ground Zero after September 11 in New York City, is intentional about exhibiting extreme focus and generosity despite overwhelming personal hardship. Six days into assisting with the disaster efforts in 2001, he was seriously injured and almost died when an 8,000-pound steel beam fell on his foot. What he went through is indescribable, and after fighting his way back from the brink, many came to know about his subsequent work when Jon Stewart devoted an episode to the shameful neglect of first responders. Feal has fought year after year for legislation that would do right by those who lost their lives that day, and in the years since, and their loved ones.

Feal said, "I'm disheartened sometimes because . . . we call ourselves the greatest nation in the world, but yet we have a strange way of repeating history and letting veterans come home from war, or 9/11 responders, or just responders now across the nation . . . they sacrifice themselves, and then we don't take care of them."

Feal openly shares about the extent of how haunted he remains, "I can block out my injury. I can block out my five days there. I can't block out the smell; [it's] probably why I don't sleep enough. When I close my eyes, I smell Ground Zero . . . This [is] not just me saying this, this is other 9/11 responders, and first responders and volunteers who will say the same thing. Especially this time of the year, when I shut my eyes, that smell comes back. And it's like it's putting its hand over my mouth and nose. And it gets tough." Amid all the suffering he still experiences physically and emotionally, his laser focus on helping others is astounding. On every level. He's gotten legislation changed. He's donated a kidney. And, every morning on a walk with his dog when getting his coffee from 7-11, he buys coffee for the person behind him. Every morning.

This ability to be intentional about *what* we're focusing on, *when*, and *how* can allow us to still move amid these modern times while not losing ourselves along the way. Intention is like the banks of a river through which grace can flow.

"Just because I have thick skin doesn't mean I'm not sensitive."

Sometimes having intention is about setting limits. Jon Lovett is a former political speechwriter and co-founder of Crooked Media. I appreciated having a tiny window into his effort to manage all he is trying to navigate when, during one of his shows, he added a segment called "The Russia Stuff," and explained: "Here's how it works. We put a two-minute clock up, because while it's good to keep up with the Russia stuff, for the most part we should be focusing on other issues—as we all say to ourselves over and over again—that we can't be distracted from *one* crazy thing because we chose the *other* crazy thing to be the thing we're not going to be distracted from. A decision I don't always understand . . . but there've been some developments and as always we don't know what to do with them. 'Oh, ok, that's terrible . . .' but then we keep moving on with our lives, so . . . two minutes on the clock! Let's begin."

Being intentional does not mean being perfect. We are talking about doing the best with what you have at your disposal, even if it's a bit messy. My daughter's godfather died when she was eleven. As David had attended her birth and remained a steadfast and adoring presence, her grief was weighty. The day after he died, she had a soccer game. Knowing my daughter was a shadow of herself I asked the coach if I could talk with him amid the hectic, pre-game scene. I told him quickly what had happened. The coach paused, and I could see his mind reeling, trying to find something, anything he could do. After a long moment he said, "Right. Okay, I'll have her play defense." And he walked away. I can honestly tell you that to this day I'm not entirely sure what he meant by that, and how that was where he landed in terms of comfort and solace. But, truly, it was comforting. Not, perhaps, a common way of responding? But we appreciate how intentional and earnest he was with trying to find *something* he could offer.

Protect your morning

Begin as you mean to go on. Each morning we have the opportunity to begin our days with the focus we hope to maintain as we go on through our day. Many traditions have as a central tenet the importance of protecting one's morning. Of course, this can be a challenge if you're an adolescent trying to get enough sleep—and staying in bed until the last minute feels critical—or if you wake up each morning to an immediately chaotic environment. This doesn't need to be an elaborate ordeal. But I do think there's some merit in not starting your day by opening your eyes and reaching for your phone—or having your alarm wake you up to the news. One study revealed that two of the biggest contributors to daily stress are hearing about what the government or politicians are doing and watching, reading, or listening to the news. Why begin our days this way? Consider a digital detox or a platform purge.

Even if all you can manage is to protect sixty seconds before you bring in the outside world, start each day by regulating your breathing and bringing to the fore of your mind one intention for the day. An achievable, practical intention. Not "May I be a good person today." Something more specific, along the lines of, "When the criticisms rush in, may I find three things to be grateful for." Or, "Should I feel my heart and mind begin to be colonized by fear, I will think about one person who inspires me." To that effect.

> "What you encounter, recognize or discover depends to a large degree on the quality of your approach. Many of the ancient cultures practiced careful rituals of approach. An encounter of depth and spirit was preceded by careful preparation . . . When we approach with reverence, great things decide to approach us. Our real life comes to the surface and its light awakens the concealed beauty in things. When we walk on the earth with reverence, beauty will decide to trust us. The rushed heart and the arrogant mind lack the gentleness and patience to enter that embrace."
>
> —John O'Donohue, poet and philosopher

One colleague I know, who lost her mother in a homicide, wrote in a journal to her, "I've been watching the Olympics. I have noticed that before the swimmers go into the water they bend down and they scoop up the water and they splash their faces and their chests vigorously. I'm sure anybody who knows the sport of swimming knows why they do this, but it's not one that I know very well. I guess I could Google it and find out the real reason, but I've made up my own narrative. It seems to me that they're trying to get adjusted to the temperature of the water before they start their swim because the last thing they want is to be in shock and have their body and their heart react as they dive into that pool. That's how I feel these days, Mom. I wish every day when I wake up in the morning I could splash myself with life so that my heart and my body wouldn't be so startled when I remember."

While starting your day with specific intention can feel contrived, having a deliberate practice around this is essential, since we're trying to traverse extremely strong forces that have been passed down through human development. Neuroscientists say, after all, that whatever fires together, wires together.

Manage volume and intensity of distractions

Once you have established intention for the day, then throughout your day be mindful about the volume and content of whatever you're bringing in to distract you, which can hamper your ability to focus. Actor and performer Mandy Patinkin said, "The biggest public mistake I ever made was that I chose to do *Criminal Minds* in the first place. I thought it was something very different. I never thought they were going to kill and rape all these women every night, every day, week after week, year after year. It was very destructive to my soul and my personality. . . . I'm not making a judgment on the taste [of people who watch crime procedurals]. But I'm concerned about the effect it has. Audiences all over the world use this programming as their bedtime story. This isn't what you need to be dreaming about."

We should be wary of the calls for alarm designed to heighten anxiety over trending issues online. Whether these are coming at us from the proliferation of industries of hate speech and propaganda that continue to foment divisiveness, or we, ourselves, are inducing anxiety among our friends and loved ones, this fear-based tactic can cause us to lose track of the core issue we were concerned about in the first place and quickly cause more damage than good. As journalist Julie Beck shares, "Anxiety is not a necessary prerequisite for action." A meta-analysis study conducted by Dr. Dolores Albarracin, a professor of psychology at the University of Illinois, found that while "inducing fear does change people's attitudes, intentions, and behaviors . . . If the message is not actionable, then you're not going to get effects overall." In other words, don't just spread stress and anxiety so others will feel it, too—propose specific actions to combat the problem at hand and enact change. Let's be intentional with what we're taking in and with what we're sharing with or asking of others.

"It keeps me from looking at my phone every two seconds."

When talking about his novel *Exit West*, author Mohsin Hamid shared about his efforts to be intentional with where he allows his mind to go and how he chooses to spend his time:

"Every parent, wherever you live in the world, there are fears that we have for our children. What happens when we drop them off to school? What happens, you know, when they're making their way home? What happens when we're not with them? And in a way, every parent is sort of dependent on the benevolence of the society around them to take care of their children.

And we get these reminders that maybe it isn't as benevolent as we'd like. But we're sort of helpless in the face of that. And that's, for me, a call to engage and to be sort of politically active because society requires each of us to intervene. It won't just be the way we want it to be.

This is something which living in Pakistan, perhaps, has taught me—and, you know, we live in a world where there is a constant feed from social media, the news, etc., of things that can scare us. And we become so anxious because human beings are meant—are designed to be sensitized to dangerous stuff. You know, you get a bad review as a writer, you remember it for 10 years. You get a hundred good reviews, you forget them all. You say hello to a hundred people in the city and it doesn't mean anything to you. One racist comment passes by, and it sticks with you a decade.

We keep the negative stuff because it's the negative stuff that's going to, you know, potentially kill us. That fin in the water—maybe it is a shark. That yellow thing behind the tree—maybe it is a lion. You need to be scared. But contemporary culture in Pakistan, just like in America, is continuously hitting us with scary stuff. And so we are utterly anxious. I think that it's very important to resist that anxiety, to think of ways of resisting the constant inflow of negative feelings, not to become depoliticized as a result but to actually work actively to bring into being an optimistic future.

And for me, writing books and being . . . someone who's politically active is part of that. I don't want to be anxious on my day-to-day life. I want to try to imagine a future I'd like to live in and then write books and do things that, in my own small way, make it more likely that that future will come to exist."

Many adults, governed by executive functioning, may understand the benefits of taking a break from technology and, even still, are challenged by trying to wean themselves. Adolescents, with brains still in development, may not yet see the value or may just not know how to disengage.

Step one may be understanding the neuroscience behind technology. Paul Lewis, U.S. West Coast bureau chief for *The Guardian*, has written extensively on this topic, and published an article titled "'Our Minds Can Be Hijacked': The Tech Insiders Who Fear a Smartphone Dystopia." In it, Nir Eyal, author and tech industry consultant, explains the subtle psychological tricks built into digital apps and sites to make people develop addictive habits—tricks like exploiting negative emotions that trigger desires for positive reinforcement, or creating cravings by varying rewards people receive online. "Feelings of boredom, loneliness, frustration, confusion and indecisiveness often instigate a slight pain or irritation and prompt an almost instantaneous and often mindless action to quell the negative sensation," according to Eyal. Sound familiar? When we feel even slightly uncomfortable, we may have become conditioned to open social media on our computers, or pick up our phones to scroll, tap, or swipe.

Addictive by design, the sites and apps we tend to visit are built with feedback loops stimulating the dopamine system. Dopamine prompts us to seek (and keep seeking) rewards, and our devices provide almost instant gratification. But I appreciate how many folks who helped create this technology are now open about the unforeseen consequences of their work. Eyal says, "The technologies we use have turned into compulsions, if not full-fledged addictions." And Loren Brichter, designer of the pull-to-refresh feature now prevalent in phone apps, shares, "Smartphones are useful tools. But they're addictive. Pull-to-refresh is addictive. . . . When I was working on them, it was not something I was mature enough to think about. I'm not saying I'm mature now, but I'm a little bit more mature, and I regret the downsides."

It's important that we be realistic about how likely it is that we can self-monitor both *how much time* we're spending online and *how* we're spending our time. Even the originators of these technologies are now taking measures to manage the volume of their distraction—installing web browser plug-ins to eradicate news feeds, having other adults put parental controls on even the adults' devices, getting apps that reward them for staying off the phone, turning off push notifications, and sending their children to schools where tech is practically banned. Eyal himself connected the router in his home to an outlet timer to cut off Internet access at a set time every day.

And as we strive to be more intentional about how we're using technology, let's remember we are not only susceptive to addictive tools—the *content* we're consuming may also be problematic. "The same forces that led tech firms to hook users with design tricks also encourage those companies to depict the world in a way that makes for compulsive, irresistible viewing," according to James Williams, an ex-Google strategist who co-founded the advocacy group Time Well Spent. "The attention economy incentivizes the design of technologies that grab our attention. In so doing, it privileges our impulses over our intentions. That means privileging what is sensational over what is nuanced, appealing to emotion, anger and outrage." He goes on to explain how and why corporations and the media are approaching content this way. "The news media is increasingly working in service to tech companies, and must play by the rules of the attention economy to sensationalize, bait, and entertain in order to survive." The barrage of content designed to retain our attention by appealing to heightened emotions could have cascading negative impact on individuals and on society. Williams also acknowledges carryover into the political realm. "[This phenomenon] is not only distorting the way we view politics but, over time, may be changing the way we think, making us less rational and more impulsive. We've habituated ourselves into a perpetual cognitive style of outrage, by internalizing the dynamics of the medium," he says.

Employing discipline and setting limits is not only self-preserving but may also help influence a positive cultural shift. I was impressed when working with a team of counter-terrorism specialists. This is a group that faces overwhelming demands *all* the time and they are, out of necessity, tied to their devices. Still, once everyone gathered for our session, the specialist in charge said, "So, for this meeting, I am going to ask everyone, including myself, to put away all technology so we can really be present." Folks seemed to let out a collective exhale when the laptops were closed and moved aside. Whether deciding to run a meeting differently or designating a tech-free day for yourself, your family, or your friends, small changes can further strengthen our internal personal agency when navigating overwhelm.

Nurture gratitude

The combo of being conscious with where we put our focus and being intentional about nurturing gratitude can be extremely powerful. Several times each week, I think about a judge I worked with years ago. Near the end of a long training session with a judges-only group, we were talking about how, practically, we can pull practices into our lives to help us sustain. And there sat the judge, surrounded by colleagues from all around the state. He spoke up, and said slowly, "I force myself to stay sitting on that bench every day after the entire courtroom has cleared out, and I make myself pour through the whole docket of what happened that day. I try to find one thing—even just a single ruling I made—that possibly alleviated harm in one child's life. If I do not do that practice every single day, I will drown in the hopelessness of all of this."

Instinctually, we know that gratitude may feel good. But science backs up the notion that gratitude has a significant impact on our overall health both individually and collectively. When we feel gratitude, parts of our brain involved in feelings of bonding and connectedness are activated, and we release neurochemicals like dopamine and serotonin. As neuroscientist Dr. Antonio Damasio says, "Gratitude rewards generosity and maintains the cycle of healthy social behavior."

Working with what is, with any amount of gratitude one can muster, can be deeply self-preserving. When asked by other gun violence survivors how he has managed, Jay Ward tells the story of visiting his physician after returning from his brother's funeral. Jay expressed that he didn't know how to go on. At all. His doctor softened his voice and said, "Jay, if after this, you can just try to live your life . . . live it well . . . that will be honoring Adam." Living well has become Jay's creed as he competes in Ironman races, works abroad, and spends time at gymnastics with his young nieces. He does not take anything for granted anymore. When Colin Warner spoke about how he's continued with his life since being exonerated after spending twenty years in prison for a crime he did not commit, he talked about focus and gratitude and shared, "My duty today is to just try to live beyond that experience."

Stepping back to appreciate that we have the sheer opportunity to contribute and have a positive impact in the world can do wonders toward helping us maintain perspective and alleviate overwhelm. I worked with an engineer, inexperienced with exposure to trauma on the job, whose role had shifted to include spending hours and hours reviewing horrific images as a content moderator. He shared, "My partner keeps commenting that I'm so happy, yet I'm seeing unspeakable things. But I think I'm happy because I feel like I'm actually helping. Like what I'm doing matters."

I also draw inspiration from a nurse I met who was very worried about her own intensifying sense of defeat. She resolved to try to do something about it, and so each shift before she left the hospital she would go to each patient and thank them for something specific from her time with them. She acknowledged sometimes she would have to dig deep but she was committed to this practice and struck by how much it helped her sustain her ability to care.

"I've never seen Archbishop Tutu miss an opportunity to thank someone."

—Douglas Abrams, author

I encourage trying a few ways of practicing gratitude, then ritualizing them into each day—whether focusing on what is going well or reminding ourselves of something we are grateful for. It can be simple. Before you drift off to sleep, and when you first wake up each morning, bring into your mind one thing you are thankful for. Many cultures and traditions use meals as a time to express gratitude for food, and often everyone gathered is invited to voice an appreciation or share a high and low point from their day. I know teachers and union leaders and journalists and CEOs who take the opportunity when their teams are gathered to invite everyone to say one thing they are grateful for. If folks start to look queasy when I talk with them about this, I assure them that they don't have to touch each other or make eye contact or light a candle in the middle of their staff meeting. Just have everyone go around and say one thing they notice that is going well. Even something this small can help us move from the reality of what is hard to the realm of what is still possible.

Employ discipline to help maintain perspective

Given the volume of demands on us, and stimuli around us, and the extremity of so much of what is unfolding around the world . . . it can, at times, feel draining to intentionally direct where our focus is as opposed to constantly playing defense against distractions in our surroundings. Be disciplined. But be gentle. It's like tuning a guitar string: Tighten too much, and it will break; too loose, it won't play.

> "There are events in our personal lives and our collective history that seem categorically irredeemable, moments in which the grounds for gratefulness and hope have sunk so far below the sea level of sorrow that we have ceased to believe they exist. But we have within us the consecrating capacity to rise above those moments and behold the bigger picture in all of its complexity, complementarity, and temporal sweep, and to find in what we see not illusory consolation but the truest comfort there is: that of perspective."
>
> —Maria Popova

Unconsciously, sometimes when I'm at a loss, my mind returns to one of the saddest moments of my life and when the intentional focus required was a saving grace. There is nothing I've wanted more in my life than to get to have children. The degree to which I wanted to have a family combined with years of doing trauma work and seeing the countless tragic things that can transpire, have made for many haunting moments. Our first daughter was eighteen months old when I became pregnant for a second time. While I had a bit less capacity for neurosis on some level—given the effort that was going into parenting as well as continuing to pursue my professions—my angst throughout pregnancy was higher given I now knew, in a very real way, what was riding on it all. The spotting began around eight weeks in. Given how OCD I was throughout each pregnancy, I did not go the bathroom a single time without saying a tiny prayer: "Please let there not be any blood." And there hadn't been. For so many times. But this time, there was. Though enveloped in that feeling of "This can't be happening, this isn't happening, it's not what I think it is. This isn't happening," within a few hours I was unceremoniously miscarrying at home. Bathroom door open, holding onto the sink, trying to steady myself through the searing pain.

My sharpest memory of the whole brutal ordeal was when our daughter appeared in the doorway of the bathroom. Her huge golden afro was backlit as the sun streamed through the hallway. She was asking for an apple.

We're home alone, my child is waiting patiently for an apple, and I'm miscarrying a pregnancy. For me, it's one of the times I can remember most in my life when focusing on something else—the seemingly less urgent—was So. Incredibly. Comforting. I pulled myself together enough to shift my focus to her request. I got to the kitchen, found an apple, washed it, cut it, and set my daughter up with her snack. I didn't know then, of course, the duration of the physical pain that would ensue, nor the complicated grief that comes with miscarrying. But I think back to that moment at times and remember the comfort that outside focus momentarily brought me, and remember that focusing on something other than that which is immediately unfolding is not a betrayal, but rather a way to hold it—all of it—in a larger space, which is, sometimes, the only thing that allows it to be bearable.

I appreciated listening to historian and author Doris Kearns Goodwin address the merit of employing discipline at a conference. She named an impressive list of U.S. presidents who would regularly write letters they never planned to send. Instead, they wrote to fully express the depth of their feelings and metabolize their experiences. That practice feels particularly poignant now, in this digital age. It often seems that maximum impulse and minimal intention go into what we say or post or tweet. Little thought goes into considering how our words may affect others.

"Maybe you shouldn't send out e-mails when you're tired."

When we maximize intention and minimize impulse, we are better positioned to make decisions that serve us for the long haul. Let's aspire to have an intimate relationship with our feelings such that we know how to channel them in a valuable and worthwhile way.

"We've got to be as clear-headed about human beings as possible, because we are still each other's only hope."

—James Baldwin

FIVE

Disconnect Less, Be Present More

When our beloved dog had cancer, we did all we could to help him be comfortable toward the end of his life. Because Rottweilers are so strong, they require a *lot* of pain medication, so we essentially had to give him what seemed like horse tranquilizers. While we were all caring for him, my daughters were in charge of giving him his daily meds. One day the girls were gone, and as I grabbed his handful of meds I thought, "When's the last time I took my stuff?" So, I gathered all my vitamins, got a glass of water, and swished down my pills. Then I turned and looked at the counter, and my vitamins were sitting there. In that moment, I realized I'd just taken all of my Rottweiler's meds.

I stood there for a minute and decided to call the vet. The vet tech on call wasn't particularly reassuring, so I called Poison Control. [Mind you, I have never had to call Poison Control before. Not for my own kids or for any children in my care. But there I was, standing in my kitchen, calling Poison Control on myself.] When the pharmacist answered the phone, I said, "I just did the stupidest thing ever," and proceeded to describe exactly what happened. There was a significant pause, and then out of her mouth came, "This happens *all* the time."

Maybe you've had one of those moments where you know that what the person trying to comfort you is saying is not entirely true. I think we can agree, this does not happen all the time: Random forty-seven-year-old women are not calling Poison Control because they're so disconnected from themselves and their immediate surroundings that they've taken their Rottweiler's medication. But in that moment, I didn't care because it was so massively reassuring to just have someone with that presence be able to remind me that I wasn't alone.

Report after report documents how—despite more technologies aimed at *connecting* people, ideas, and information—people of all ages continue to experience greater and greater social and personal *disconnection*. Why? Well, our body, mind, and spirit can only keep up with so much. When overloaded, we may disconnect because it all *is* too much or *feels like* it is too much. Disconnecting from our self and our immediate surroundings may have been a conscious or unconscious strategy from back in the day that helped us to get through. But if we don't tend to those circumstances, past and present, and if we don't constantly hone our ability to remain connected to ourselves, even amid what may feel untenable, we may unconsciously or consciously disconnect. And disconnection from ourselves can creep in gradually, stealthily, because of what we choose to expose ourselves to or happen to be exposed to. I spoke with an eighteen-year-old in the wake of a terrorist attack, and when I asked how she was managing she replied, "I try not to think too much about it. At least right now. If I do, it would all be too much." This self-awareness is a gift. While it is true that there are times when gaining a little distance (even from our own selves) may be helpful, it is critical we bring a tenacious awareness to these moments with an intention of reconnecting fully and preemptively as soon as we are able.

What does this look like? When we are disconnected and not deliberate, we are often numb. We check out, we're detached. We go through the motions and are more inclined to act with a lack of integrity. Not bringing our full presence to bear can have detrimental consequences for us and can immensely impact our interactions and relationships with others.

"What it's come to for me is . . . I spend a significant amount of time every day at work, walking slowly down the halls or taking the stairs instead of the elevator, so I have time to remind myself and just say over and over to myself, 'Don't be a dick. Don't be a dick. Don't be a dick.' "

—Nurse

Fortunately, when we practice being present—conscious—we can quiet the overwhelm. A friend of mine who is a lawyer for a major U.S. tech company in China said after the death of his mother, "Present?! I don't want to be present! I want to be the farthest fucking thing from present. Anything but present." But when we flinch, judge, manipulate, or disconnect from that which feels intolerable, we miss the opportunity to metabolize that discomfort and transform it. We can aspire to stay engaged with our thoughts and feelings and not be thrown off by inner turbulence. Of course, part of the process is recognizing and acknowledging places and times in our lives when we are not connected . . .

Disconnected?

Part of why we care about keeping a close eye on if we are disconnected is that when we are disconnected we cannot reliably gauge if we are doing harm. A residential juvenile corrections worker shared with me, "The kids all say, including my own, that I'm like the Tin Man. I have no heart."

Time and again, I see that the sequence of harm starts, and can be interrupted, within us. Even while we're trying to show up and do right by others, care for others, tend to small and large issues locally and out in the world, so often our ability to do that *and* tend to our blood pressure, *and* keep an eye on our moods, *and* generally treat our bodies well . . . falls by the wayside. The next step: Harm arises in our intimate relationships, whether with family members or friends. As author and professor of law Sheryll Cashin stated, "There are consequences for the children of activists." Finally, often harm arises in our more public selves. Time and again we learn we absolutely cannot show up and help repair the world *out there* while allowing harm *in here.* By the time we are the absolute jerk at school or the coworker folks avoid at all costs, a lot of harm has already happened much closer to home.

"Your inability to turn off your critical voice, combined with your fear of disappointing your overbearing, demanding father, is causing you to lose faith in your fastball."

Another significant consequence of being disconnected is that we won't be able to bring our quality of presence to bear. This matters in tiny, daily moments, as well as rare, epic times. Time and again in life we learn that even when we can't affect the outcome of a given situation, our presence can mean the difference between creating harm or escalating suffering or slightly shifting or absolutely transforming whatever is unfolding. Sometimes our ability to be present is, literally, all we have.

You know what I'm talking about, yes? Perhaps you've been in a vulnerable situation, when even if the ultimate outcome could not and would not change—the school suspension was going to stay the school suspension, the home foreclosure was going to stay the home foreclosure, the diagnosis was going to stay the diagnosis—the other human being involved with access to resources, information, or authority (the head of school or the accountant or the doctor) was able to be present, make eye contact, and treat you with dignity. That person's ability to calmly bear witness had an enormous impact in terms of minimizing suffering and shifting an experience that could have caused harm to one of hardship instead.

A seventeen-year-old family friend reminded me just how deeply this matters when describing how isolated she felt in society at large, despite being surrounded by many loved ones. During her first year of high school, she lost a dear friend to suicide. Almost a year later, her father took his own life. She waded through trauma-filled days, yet high school still required her attention and her job still hoped for her return. "We are all now dealing with things that kids our age should never have to go through but we all do. There are these things in life you have to grapple with—and then, a month later, you're expected to take the SAT. I think a lot of people are able to be sympathetic, but not empathetic. There are so many different planes you're operating on that don't even connect. It's like you can't even fathom it all belongs in the same world."

I have seen on many occasions how unique work environments can be conducive to fostering either the best or the worst in employees. It is evident that airline call center workers, TSA agents, airport security, flight attendants, and others in the travel industry, for example, are among those who are often extremely overwhelmed by the stress of their work. But for Jay Ward, the presence of airline industry workers made a significant and long-lasting impact during the first few critical hours after his brother was murdered. That day, employee after employee brought their presence to bear.

During the call when he learned of Adam's death, though he could not make out much from his utterly distraught parents, he clearly heard their pleading to "Please come home right away. Please." Jay and his sister lived in different cities—both across the country from their parents—but when a friend contacted the airlines on Jay's behalf, the personnel on duty that day did everything in their power to help. Seats on flights were secured such that Jay and his sister could meet on the first connecting flight possible. Airline escorts met them at the airport, ushered them through security, and took them to a room where they could wait before boarding. Canceled flights and missed connections later, each airline and airport representative did all they could to move them through the various airports seamlessly—over tarmacs and through concourses—all the while trying to screen them from the countless television screens in each airport that were reporting on and replaying the shooting over and over and over. On the last leg to their parents' home, the plane was filled with journalists and reporters traveling both to cover the story and to pay respect to their fallen comrades. The flight attendants stood watch over Jay and his sister to assure there would be no unwanted contact and handed them off to loved ones waiting at their home airport.

Jay has shared with me stories about the many, many people who helped him and his family survive this loss. But there is something particularly moving in the way he talks about each of those strangers in the airline industry. Perhaps it's because they weren't childhood friends, their family pastor, their neighbors, or their current community. Perhaps it was because each of those people—who helped Jay and his sister traverse the country as quickly as possible during an impossibly heartbreaking day—were drawing purely on their sense of humanity. There was no distracting debate on guns or discussion of workplace safety or anything else. Person after person was rooted in their ability to bring their presence to bear on behalf of those who were suffering, thereby acting with acute decency and honoring a family's dignity.

For years after a hard time, we can reflect on how events unfolded, and sometimes what we remember most is one person who made such a difference in that moment, for better or worse. Whether in formal or informal roles, we each have countless opportunities throughout our days to bring this quality of presence to bear. We have the capacity to be this presence for the people we encounter in our life.

Practice being present

The good news here is that disconnection is so often remediable. We have an internal ecosystem that unequivocally needs to be tended to. When we pull in our attention to take care of our minds and bodies, it becomes more natural to engage and be present. And once we've stabilized our internal systems and become more grounded, physically and chemically, it is much easier to quiet our minds and be more conscious in our circumstances.

Detox

First, a dedicated, daily practice of detoxing is called for. How do you do that? There are limitless options. One of the places to start is by eliminating or limiting those things in our life that may be toxic, addictive, deleterious. Whether alcohol, drugs, refined sugar, caffeine, nicotine, highly processed food, or, of course, screens. Also, drink more water. Easier said than done, I know. Take one step at a time. Less is more.

"Look, you seem nice, and I don't want to hurt your feelings, but I was really drunk when we met, got married and bought this house."

One of my favorite moments talking with folks about this was during a discussion with a large group about what it would be like to try to go for twenty-four hours without some of what many of us depend on. I started by qualifying that I wasn't talking about your cocktail hour (which might be getting earlier and earlier each day) or if you get high regularly or any pharmaceuticals you might be on in a non-mindful way. I'm just talking about going for twenty-four hours without caffeine, sugar, nicotine, and highly processed food. Lots of folks burst into laughter at what seemed like the absurdity of such a notion, and one of their community members who did not share their sense of humor commanded the attention of the entire group when she said, completely seriously, "Oh . . . so . . . basically, you're asking us to fast."

There are any number of habits we all have that may not qualify as addictions, but the thought of going without them for any amount of time makes us very, very uneasy. You may have even experienced this when you can't find your phone . . . for even five minutes. You start to sweat and feel that sick feeling in your stomach. Be aware when that happens; perhaps take steps to wean yourself a bit?

In terms of detoxing from screens, the folks I know who are the most pained by constantly monitoring the news are those who are doing so in the spirit of being prepared. Those who may be the target of racism or xenophobia or any kind of current supremacy that would have one fearing for one's safety, life, or the well-being of loved ones may not have the privilege to disengage entirely from their screens. The indescribable burden on these folks is crushing. I've talked to international online safety specialists, immigration advocates, and civil rights lawyers who have proposed a designated driving-type agreement with peers, so the responsibility of constant monitoring could be shared by each person taking a shift, reducing everyone's overall exposure.

Engage your breath: Meditation and yoga

Once we've brought some discretion to what we're already taking in, then we can consider what we might add to help metabolize and mitigate overwhelm. In terms of maximum efficiency and effectiveness, simply engaging one's breath is at the heart of many ancient practices and traditions as a tool to help regulate our nervous systems and to deepen our ability to work with our mind. In modern times, Giancarlo Esposito, known for his role on *Breaking Bad*, said of meditation and yoga, "It has saved my life—probably saved me from me because it's allowed me a deeper connection to be able to give me a little distance from not only the things that may trouble me, but from a very busy mind. . . . We are thinkers, we are intellectual people, many of us. . . . for me to turn that switch off, meditation really helps."

Key to this part of the practice is finding a centering solution that works for you and being open to adapt as what works for you evolves. My cousin-in-law Jonah Lipsky has spent years studying meditation, including assisting with a study at Brown University that reminds us that sometimes people have difficult experiences during meditation or afterward. There are times when, instead of sitting, moving mindfully may be better for us—whether that is practicing tai chi, qigong, or even walking slowly and mindfully.

Another example of moving mindfully, yoga, has been found to contribute to healthy neural development and long-term memory, as well as leading to a significant reduction in symptoms of post-traumatic stress, including fewer intrusive thoughts and less dissociation from the body. Dr. Bessel van der Kolk states, "Agency starts with what scientists call interoception, our awareness of our subtle sensory, body-based feelings: the greater that awareness, the greater our potential to control our lives. Knowing *what* we feel is the first step to knowing *why* we feel that way. If we are aware of the constant changes in our inner and outer environment, we can mobilize to manage them."

Be active

It is beneficial to be active. Whenever you can. However you can. In your mind. Body. Spirit.

Kanin

"I'm glad to see that almost everyone has been taking advantage of the new executive fitness center."

Physical ability level, finances, time—none of these need be barriers. Engaging one's breath mindfully and deliberately—with an intention of ensuring nothing becomes stagnant within our nervous system—can be done through as diverse a range as prayer and chanting or playing the saxophone and dancing. There are endless options. Unless medically advised against physical exertion, if one is able, elevating one's heart rate and breaking a sweat has been shown to have concrete and lasting benefits. Find what works for you and make it part of your daily practice. Here's why.

Exercise, even a brisk walk, increases energy levels and boosts serotonin in the brain, which contributes to heightened mental clarity, which will allow you to be more present. In singer-songwriter Bruce Springsteen's autobiography he bravely reveals areas of his life that have been challenging, including his continuous struggles with anxiety and depression, and discusses the therapeutic nature of being such a physically exerting musician. He notes that when you are "exhausted well beyond the reach of your anxieties, [you can be] finally and blessedly present."

Feeling overwhelmed is a common symptom of anxiety, and American Psychological Association studies have shown that regular exercise has the potential to decrease anxiety simply by desensitizing people to symptoms that can be present both during physical exertion or a panic attack or an episode of generalized anxiety, such as increased heart rate, quickness of breath, and heavy perspiration. As a result, anxiety and overwhelm can be less frightening or debilitating when it occurs. I talked to a college student who had been struggling with severe social anxiety. A fierce athlete, she shared, "Sometimes I'll feel my sore muscles and think about what I am able to do on the track and then I tell myself if I can do that, I can walk across campus and make eye contact with people."

If that's not enough to persuade you, consider this: People who do regular physical activity have a 30 percent lower risk of early death. I appreciate the thoughtfulness so many are putting into reframing our thinking about exercise. Exercise is Medicine, for example, is an initiative started by the American College of Sports Medicine that has expanded globally to encourage health care providers to evaluate patients' level of physical activity at every visit and provide guidelines, counsel, and resources to help patients improve their physical fitness. The fact that folks are being explicit about exercise being *medicine* is inspiring. If you count yourself among the many individuals who tend to start and stop exercise, struggling to maintain a routine, then viewing exercise as medicine—as preventative care or treatment—may be a helpful frame. Prioritize it the best you can. Find a system to remember to do it. Try to see it as an opportunity, not a burden. And should you miss it once or twice or several times, no problem! Try again.

Sleep

Researchers are also doubling down on how important sleep is to support our ability to be present during our waking hours.

Without sleep, the brain is unable to clear out toxins and clean the fluid in neuron channels at the rate necessary to maintain high-functioning, day-to-day activity, according to a study from the University of Rochester. Getting rid of toxins strengthens our immune system and allows our cells, tissues, and muscles to repair themselves. Dr. Charles Czeisler, physician and sleep researcher at Harvard Medical School, said that this is the "first direct experimental evidence at the molecular level" for why we need to sleep.

To a person, adolescents I have interviewed have told me how much they crave sleep, and yet sleep still often eludes them. They spoke over each other in a group on this subject: "The darkness is scary. I have to listen to something to fall asleep. I mean, how many times are you just alone with yourself . . . I have to have podcasts going, like, all night, otherwise I just think and think and think . . . and then I feel even more overwhelmed. We have so many distractions in our days—crutches we use to not be present with ourselves—it's hard not to do it at night, too. I get stuck in my own head so much, I feel like I'm going crazy. Being alone gets really hard, even when it's to go to sleep."

If getting the amount of sleep you need (we are all different in this regard) remains a challenge, experts I've learned from encourage two strategies: Seek outside help (from Western or Eastern fields), and schedule your sleep. Even if the homework is not done, the house isn't clean, or the episode you're watching isn't over. For this week or this month or this trial period, prioritize sleep and plan accordingly.

Go outside

Spending time in nature can also have a cleansing effect on one's mind and, in many cultures, is considered a form of preventative medicine. Forest environments are shown to decrease cortisol levels, blood pressure, and sympathetic nervous system activity. A study conducted in Japan demonstrated the unassailable power nature has on our physical and mental health. Those who participated in "forest bathing" had significantly lower heart rates and reported higher levels of relaxation and decreased levels of stress than those who walked in an urban environment. Walking in nature has also been linked with increased working memory performance and decreased anxiety, rumination, and negative affect.

NATURE WALK

There is evidence, too, that exposure to microbiomes in dirt may boost our immune systems and elevate moods. Pediatric neurologist and author Dr. Maya Shetreat-Klein shares, "In treating my patients, I want to understand the root cause of their problems . . . What I have learned is that ultimately, it all begins with dirt. . . . The bio-terrain inside of our bodies is connected intricately to the eco-terrain outside our bodies." She also explains the antidepressant effects of dirt. "Soil reaches into our bodies and brains when we get dirty in nature. If you feel wonderful when you're gardening or hiking, it may be in part because *Mycobacterium vaccae*, a soil microbe that enters your body through your nasal tract or small cuts in your skin, boosts serotonin."

While the scientific evidence is gaining on the anecdotal, even within Western medicine there is a growing movement to send people outside as a cure. Through Park Prescription programs, physicians in dozens of countries are writing prescriptions instructing patients to spend a prescribed amount of time in nature using parks, trails, and, simply, open spaces. In some cases, health care providers are distributing free park passes thanks to partnerships with state and national park services, public land agencies, and community partners. We don't have to scale mountains or ride rapids to benefit from being outside, though. Being outside for a few minutes, looking at a tree, and observing the light filtering through leaves can regulate your nervous system and allow you to be more present.

Spend time with animals

The incredibly positive impact that animals can have on people in stressful circumstances continues to move me. Even though I worked with our beloved Rottweiler, Caleb, for years as a therapy dog, I still didn't totally connect the dots on how universally animals are incorporated as support for folks during times of overwhelm. I first recognized this when reading a long article about Olympic athletes. The athletes were asked to describe the most grueling things about their training and the games themselves and then what they were most looking forward to about finally going home. When asked what they missed the most, athlete after athlete said, "My dog." And in my workshops, when a discussion is happening around what workers rely on to renew themselves, without fail a small percentage will say something about humans in their lives, but a large percentage consistently say, "My dog."

"Yes, yes, yes, I miss you, too, honey. Now put the dog on."

Time with animals is not to be underestimated. It's proven to be physiologically stimulating—reducing stress hormones and raising levels of beta endorphins, oxytocin, and dopamine. Whether you nap with your cat, volunteer in the field of equine therapy, choose a workplace that welcomes dogs, or simply pause when you see a bird outside your window, connecting with other species can be deeply regenerating.

SIX

Less Attachment, More Curiosity

As I approached the Canadian border late one night, I contemplated the reason I would give for my visit. I had been invited to work with a hospice team in a small First Nations community the next morning, but working in other countries can really hold one up at the border. I decided to tell the truth, though "vacationing" was a tempting answer.

The border agent in the booth opened his little window and asked some benign questions; he seemed quite lovely. Then he asked why I was visiting Canada. I said, "I'm going to be working in one of your communities." He looked at me, and in an instant, everything shifted. It was as if I were presumed—immediately—to be guilty. Suddenly then, I thought, "How many bags of heroin have I swallowed? How many dead bodies are in my car?" I was awash with dread.

The agent peppered me with question after question. The content of his queries was legit, but his demeanor was . . . rough. His level of intensity was so disproportionate for the situation at hand, and after a long series of questions, which I answered thoroughly and politely, he said, "Okay, we need you to go inside the building."

That's always a bad sign. Inside didn't look promising. I saw one border patrol agent at the computer, a lot of border patrol agents standing around, and a long line of very nervous-looking people. After a long wait, as they called my name, the gentleman from the booth switched places with the agent at the counter. I had been forever in a queue, only to face the person I'd spoken to in the first place.

The border agent, however, didn't skip a beat. He was still abrupt. Totally agro. I patiently gave him my handouts, showed him my website, provided contact information for the First Nations elders . . . and all the while he remained off-the-charts intense. Then he disappeared for at least five minutes, and returned, saying, gruffly, "You're free to go." I mustered a thank you and turned to walk away. Of course, my first reaction was to scan for a suggestion box where I could leave constructive customer feedback, but after a second of consideration I forced myself to head toward the door. I was only a foot and a half down the counter—barely two steps away—when he said, "Excuse me just one second."

As I took in a deep breath, thinking "Please, no," he leaned over the counter. Two inches from my face. He looked me right in the eye and he said softly and slowly, "The work you do is so interesting."

Click. Suddenly, he was Mr. Sunshine. So sweet. So kind. I had no idea where *this* guy was a foot and a half back where his other manifestation interviewed me with such severity, but this guy was completely different. He started telling me all about his extensive military service, how half the men he served with had committed suicide, and of the work they're doing to reduce the stigma in Canada around PTSD. He asked if I would be willing to do training for his coworkers. I offered to give him a case of my books which I'd brought for the training the next day—but apparently, he'd taken the time to purchase one online while I had been waiting, sweating, in the holding area. He sent me off with a huge hug. My new bestie.

You know, in some of our professions, we try to turn ourselves off and on, like a flip of the switch. Deeply identified with our sense of self, ego operating at full throttle, we may adopt a persona to wield control over others or the tasks at hand. That border agent scooched down like a foot and a half and he literally seemed like a different human being. I have no idea who he takes home. I have no idea who shows up at his kid's school. I have no idea who he is with people who have darker skin than I do or are from different countries. But the attachment he appeared to have to the power of his authority was palpable. And then he moved down the counter a bit and turned that guy off. I had no idea who he would be after I left.

Being in touch with our attachment can help us calibrate better. Our degree of intensity, our tone, our pacing—whatever it is we're doing around strangers we encounter or those known to us—we can ensure that our response is in sync with the situation. Without constant calibration, we may respond in ways out of proportion to the moment. And that disproportionate response has consequences. By checking in with ourselves, interrupting a cavalier state, and letting go of attachment, we can be the person we want to be out in the world *and* when we get home.

Our mind is like a sorting machine, taking in experiences and filing them as familiar or unfamiliar, good or bad—evaluating a new acquaintance as friend or foe. The more saturated we become, the more that sorting machine goes into overdrive, casting quick judgments. That, too, is a sign of attachment. But there isn't just one truth. When we release our grip, let go of the need to control, step out of our own way, and shift our perspective by adopting an air of curiosity, we can soothe feelings of overwhelm by relaxing into our experience moment to moment.

Of course, it's not as easy as just letting go. The practice of dissolving attachment was once described to me as being open to hearing *all* the notes in an octave, not just the notes on the scale of our own experience (the ones that we repeat). When grasping, we fixate on the notes of a familiar scale; when rejecting, we don't even hear unfamiliar notes. Only when we let the music wash over and through us does it take care of itself. Through being curious, we grant ourselves permission to let down our guard and appreciate the full score of our lives.

"Attachment is the root of suffering."

—Thich Nhat Hanh

Attached?

When assessing overwhelm, let's pay close attention to how much attachment we feel in our life. The content of our experience is often not our biggest problem, it's the activity—the attachment—around it that's the issue.

Attachment presents in many ways. We may be attached to our identity—whether that is as a border patrol agent, a community organizer, or a caretaker; whether it's about being popular at school or serving in the military; or if we identify as a parent or a surgeon or a manager. There's an edge to distinguish here between pride and perspective about one's role versus *attachment*. It's the distinction between a sense of, "I show up every day, I do the best I can, but this doesn't define me" and those of us who have more of a clenched jaw when talking about how we make our way through the world—either because we are fiercely attached to our identity or, sometimes, because our "identity" eludes us.

"I didn't get where I am by trying to please."

For a time, I joked with folks I worked with that if they were, for example, tattooing the logo of their organization on their bicep . . . that's a whole different orientation. And what can come from that might be both increased passion for the work at hand as well as increased vulnerability over time to being impacted. But then I worked with a community and a woman said, "You know, you're joking about this whole tattoo thing, but just two weeks ago I did get a tattoo of the work I'm doing." She paused a moment and said, "It would have been really helpful if you had come and done this training, you know, three weeks ago?!"

When we become attached to our identity and apply a storyline to it, we set ourselves up. We may need to untangle to gain a healthier perspective. Our club swim coach even instructs eager, dedicated young athletes, "Swimming is what you do; it's not who you are."

A particularly instructive moment came after the son of our friends Tina and Mark Lilly fell from a very, very tall tree. Their ten-year-old had suffered several life-threatening injuries from the fall, and his family and extended community spent long days in the ICU holding vigil, hoping and praying he'd live. Felix was an accomplished musician, an excellent student, involved in many activities in the community. His family supported Felix's various and time-consuming activities, but their top priority never wavered: to instill in their children their core values to be gracious, humble, and grateful. Excruciating weeks passed after his fall until one day, after being entirely unresponsive and in a coma, he smiled when his younger sister walked into the room. Felix was back. In the days that followed, with so much of who he was no longer available to him, what prevailed was his tender spirit that steadily surfaced through his smiles and, eventually, his consistent thank you's and please's to every person who helped him. As we invest time in school, sports, our artistic endeavors, and our work, it is worth continuing to remind ourselves who are we underneath all of that. If it all got stripped away, what would surface?

Another way attachment may surface is an increase in rigid behavior and dogmatic thinking. We notice a decrease in our humility. We crave a sense of having ground under our feet and, for some, that means sinking into a sense of good/bad/right/wrong/you're with me or against me. This dynamic can surface around issues like parenting or arise in dynamics between couples, friend groups, or communities. Sadly, there is no shortage of examples of how close-mindedness is surfacing in small and large ways all around the world with dire consequences. Of course, close-mindedness, a militant matrix of defenses, is often based in fear.

I often think about what a counselor said to my daughter: "As people, we connect around our vulnerabilities." Of course, to be vulnerable, we must be able to tolerate feeling afraid. For many of us, that experience of feeling fear in our bodies is daunting, so we welcome the opportunity to move into our heads, where we can gain temporary relief thinking about something in a way that provides us comfort. Even if that means simply agreeing with ourselves.

Becoming attached to our valuation of our own success can derail us when we place too much importance on how much we are doing, how much people expect or rely on us to do it, or what other people think about what we are doing. When we prioritize our *own* success over action to serve a greater cause.

"Any improvement since I brought the balloon?"

During my years in this work, I have heard countless stories from good people who have dropped the thread (at least temporarily) in terms of what they are doing and why, because of the static that can be caused by alternative storylines about what they are doing and why. One doctor I worked with whose work had been embroiled in controversy to the point of it being Breaking News shared, "I'm better now than before any of this happened, but that's because I've spent the last year really, really working on myself." She paused and continued, "There's nothing like walking through the airport and seeing your face on CNN."

Another way I have experienced attachment causing widespread damage is through greed. Whether we see small ripples of greed in our life or the larger and devastating entrenchment of values and interpretation of rights that embolden entire industries—often complicit in destruction of human life, the environment, and democracies—honest and continuous conversations with ourselves about our own greed are critical. Sometimes we feel entitled to status or access to resources or power over others—feelings that may have begun as inclinations but may now have calcified into attachment. If our internal greed is in any way manifesting itself in behavior causing harm, it's critical to hold up for a second and explore what off-ramps are available.

I have found that the stance of "I am just acting on my piece/I have no connection to the outcomes of the process"—what so many people say as they keep kicking a situation further into the system—leads to compartmentalized, dehumanized, unaccountable actions. There can be huge consequences when people don't assume accountability for the outcomes of their actions, even though all those little actions may be accumulating into bigger and more dire consequences to the people who are caught up in the system. A friend of mine who is a leader in addressing the growing crisis of exploited children around the world shares, "We get so used to trying to change things and failing that we will sometimes just stand back and watch—even when we know it's a disaster. It's very dehumanizing and it can destroy an organization's spirit. Collectively, we might be able to turn a situation around, but alone we cannot." Letting go of accountability can happen when we lose hope. As founder and director of the Equal Justice Initiative Bryan Stevenson reminds us, "Injustice prevails when hopelessness persists."

Practice being curious

When we think about how to address attachment, I am reminded of Buddhism's emphasis on having a beginner's mind or cultivating an attitude of openness and eagerness without preconceived notions. Making space for new experiences and welcoming them with a posture of curiosity and generosity, without pretending to be in control.

While we may think of children as generally more curious than adults, we know there are circumstances that can undermine their willingness to be open to new experiences in which they don't have control. Kevin Ashworth, co-founder of the NW Anxiety Institute, talks about the "illusion of control and certainty" that smartphones offer anxious young people desperate to manage their environments. "Teens will go places if they feel like they know everything that will happen, if they know everyone who will be there, if they can see who's checked in online, but life doesn't always come with that kind of certainty, and they're never practicing the skill of rolling with the punches, of walking into an unknown or awkward social situation and learning that they can survive it." We would all benefit from practicing these skills early and often.

"I would love to live like a river flows, carried by the surprise of its own unfolding."

—John O'Donohue

Dropping into our bodies can be helpful. It can be as simple as this: When feeling a tightening within, try to slowly exhale, drop your shoulders, relax your jaw, and take a moment to close and open your hands a few times. Such a small exercise can be done in the classroom or in the boardroom or on the phone or when in traffic. It doesn't have to be dramatic.

"I find the yoga helps me to be more irritating."

Foster humility

There is also great virtue in being grounded in humility. Humility seems particularly important to practice when we feel we have expertise in something. When we cultivate a sense of humility, we can reduce those moments when we dismiss others by the conceit that "I know what it's like to be a teen," "I know what it's like to be a parent," "I know what it's like to do this job." Humility allows us to be good at something and still be open to all that we have yet to learn. Preserving our willingness and capacity to be corrected or surprised keeps us flexible, lets us experience the satisfaction of learning something new, and helps us avoid the trap of binary thinking.

Filmmaker Ken Burns, who has produced and directed some of the most acclaimed historical documentaries ever made, has described the significance of crafting his documentary on Vietnam with an open mind. "The biggest thing to drop is certainty. Because I think this is what we do all the time, particularly today . . . we're always really certain . . . we're all in our hardened silos of being absolutely sure that we know what 'it' is. And there's some incredible release that takes place when you let that go."

In an interview with former lieutenant general and ambassador to NATO Doug Lute, Tommy Vietor, former spokesperson for the National Security Council and cofounder of Crooked Media, said, "You've served 35 years in the Army, you've served in the White House managing two wars, you've overseen multiple surges, you've worked at NATO as an ambassador . . . you've seen the full field in a way I think very few people who aren't the President of the United States do. Are there lessons we should learn about when, why, and how to conduct wars going forward, and maybe not make some of the mistakes you've talked about . . . how do we do this better?"

Lieutenant General Lute replied, "I'm still unpacking my last decade, you know it takes a while to decompress . . . and get your thoughts together. Here are three that are in my short, early list of my personal lessons. Number one: No shortcuts on strategy." Then he explained how in the military doctrine the word *strategy* refers to the combination of ends, ways, and means (goals, methods, and resources);

but when we take a shortcut, without figuring out how exactly we're going to do something or assembling the resources necessary to get it done, we set ourselves up for failure. He went on. "Number two: You've really got to go to school on this. You've got to master this subject." Dedicated, focused, long-term attention on strategy is critical. And the third lesson? "The last lesson is simply that even though you've got four tours in Afghanistan, or you've been doing this for ten years, or you're an intelligence professional and you've been doing this for twenty years and you speak the language, you better have a little humility. Because in my experience, when you begin to think you know everything about a problem set, you're about to be ambushed. You're about to be ambushed with circumstances, facts, conditions, changing situations that you didn't expect. And only if you're humble enough to appreciate that you're never going to know it all, are you really on safe ground."

"Watch out for his being better at boxing than you."

Laszlo Bock, former senior vice president of People Operations at Google, cites humility as one of the top attributes he looks for in candidates, but he admits that humility can be hard to find among successful people. Because they rarely experience failure, they don't know how to learn from it. "Without humility, you are unable to learn," Bock notes.

To foster greater humility, try to learn something new in an arena where you can automatically cut yourself some slack. For example, perhaps you are not already skilled in playing guitar, sketching, writing screenplays, or participating in improv. Strive to learn *something* with a bit of levity, self-compassion, and grace and then translate that posture of not presuming to know and feeling free to ask for help whenever you can, however you can, to other realms of your life.

Clarify intentions

As curiosity applies to our work, we can strive to be less attached to results and instead shift our attention to the intention with which we are doing the work. When we reframe—repeatedly—what it is we are doing and why, we will interrupt the haunting sense that we're never doing enough or that we always should be doing more.

During the Freedom Vote for Governor campaign in the fall of 1963, scores of students went to Mississippi as volunteers for the Mississippi Summer Project. The campaign, also known as Freedom Summer, was launched to attempt to register as many black voters as possible in Mississippi. Here's an excerpt from a memo sent to campaign coordinators from the committee on the ground in Jackson, Mississippi:

```
The great majority of the students came down with the
attitude, 'I know I am only going to be here for a
very short period of time, but I am willing to help in
whatever way you think I can.' There were some students,
however, who came to Mississippi with fixed ideas about
what they wanted to do and what they hoped to achieve.
```

And here is a description of their ideal volunteer candidate:

```
It is essential that an applicant possess a learning
attitude toward work in Mississippi. This is not to
discourage ingenuity or creativity; it means that an
applicant must have some understanding that his role
will only be a stopgap one: that the movement will have
to continue after he leaves and that his role will be to
work with local leadership, not to overwhelm it. He can
only do this if he shows some respect for what has gone
```

before him and an understanding of what must continue
after he leaves. He must be capable of understanding
that the success of the Mississippi movement depends on
the development of those who live and will remain in the
state. A student who seems determined to carve his own
niche, win publicity and glory when he returns home can
only have harmful effects on the Mississippi program.

Particularly when we are tackling large problems where success seems incremental at best and hard to measure, it can be seductive to become stuck on what we are doing and how we are doing it as opposed to being focused on why and to what end. U.S. Senator Cory Booker challenged the University of Pennsylvania class of 2017 with these words: "We can never allow our inability to do *everything* to undermine our determination to do *something*." Our individual desire to witness results is often not a crucial part of the collective process of creating meaningful change. Writer and historian Rebecca Solnit shares, "Most victories will be temporary, or incomplete, or compromised in some way . . . When activists mistake heaven for some goal at which they must arrive, rather than an idea to navigate by, they burn themselves out . . . don't believe that the moon is useless unless we land on it." Contributing most skillfully to things within our individual control is one way we can make progress on those things that remain only in our collective control.

This applies to our planet as well. One of my teachers told me about monks in Thailand who, along with villagers, have ordination ceremonies where they tie brilliantly colored orange robes on the trees to raise others' awareness of their sacredness and thus stop or slow deforestation. To focus on doing things is to contribute, but understanding one might not be able to see the outcome, and refusing to become daunted when you don't, can free you to being present for doing what you can, when you can, even if seemingly small. I appreciated the reminder of this from my friend who had just started at university. Having spent a lot of time outdoors growing up, she was not a stranger to appreciating one's environment, but one of her first classes at school was on the climate crisis. She'd only been away a month when she planned a quick trip home for the weekend. Counting down the days until her arrival, her mother asked for flight information so she could pick her up at the airport. Her text message reply was immediate and resolute. "Mom! Global warming! I'm taking the light rail home."

Photo by A. Lipsky. Santa Marta, Colombia

In *Hope in the Dark*, Rebecca Solnit writes, "Make yourself one small republic of unconquered spirit. . . . If your activism is already democratic, peaceful, creative, then in one small corner of the world these things have triumphed."

There is merit in being deeply curious about what our goals are and what "success" means. Life involves risk. We must determine what components of the risk are in our individual control and what are out of our individual control. We act efficaciously with the elements in our control, and we are accountable for the impact of the choices we make in our control.

Because many of us have authority over other people's lives (how we interact with our children or loved ones, who to charge with a crime, whose kids to put into foster care, who gets the scholarship, which therapy will help), it is important for us to be efficacious—to have merited confidence in our methods and to have a burden of benefit in our actions. Simply doing for the sake of doing, when our doing has consequences for others, is insufficient. The way to be efficacious is by decreasing our attachment to "being right" or doing things a certain way and instead being more curious about the intelligence in what people are already doing, what conditions are at play, what is contributing to those conditions, and how to mitigate harm.

> "Do not depend on the hope of results. . . . You may have to face the fact that your work will be apparently worthless and even achieve no result at all, if not perhaps results opposite to what you expect. As you get used to this idea, you start more and more to concentrate not on the results but on the value, the rightness, the truth of the work itself."
>
> —Thomas Merton, Trappist monk and writer

These principles also extend, to a degree, beyond individual expectations to structural expectations. For those of us who are pragmatists, there is a very tender balance between remaining inspired and fueled by what is possible while staying grounded in a compassionate realism. Activists, lawyers, and others in and outside of Syria, for example, have spent years collecting evidence of atrocities and war crimes committed against the Syrian people. But justice is a long-term prospect. It may be many more years before perpetrators are brought to trial. Kevin Jon Heller, a professor of criminal law at the University of London, said, "We can have some hope that there is eventually going to be a time of reckoning . . . we really need to temper our expectations and . . . our criteria of success for international criminal justice. Because that to me is the danger: Expecting it to do too much too quickly and then only being disappointed in what it fails to do."

Be self-respecting and discerning

We seek to find equilibrium in terms of striving for what we want and being self-respecting in terms of what we know (and our respective areas of competence), while *also* being able to truly empathize with others and recognize that "what I *don't* know about this is everything." Our aim is to strike the balance between having a beginner's mind and not being attached—and having humility, while not handing over our minds and brains to others.

As singer and writer Rosanne Cash said, "Persist and verify . . . The power that we abdicate to others out of our insecurity—to others who insult us with their faux-intuition or their authoritarian smugness—that comes back to hurt us so deeply . . . But the power we wrest from our own certitude—that saves us."

When we persist and verify we undermine our collective tendency to believe we know more than we actually do, while simultaneously giving ourselves permission not to pretend to know things that we don't. This practice gives us an antidote to the "illusion of explanatory depth." Cognitive scientists and professors Steven Sloman and Philip Fernbach did a study about how sociability impacts the function of the human mind. They confirmed that otherwise informed people often rely on other people's expertise and agree with [potentially baseless] opinions because they have become dependent on other minds. "This is how a community of knowledge can become dangerous," they write. "As a rule, strong feelings about issues do not emerge from deep under-standing." Sloman and Fernbach see in this result an opportunity. "If we—or our friends, or the pundits—spent less time pontificating and more trying to work through the implications of policy proposals, we'd realize how clueless we are and moderate our views."

And in our personal relationships, shining a light of self-respecting curiosity upon one's temperament from both a nature and nurture standpoint can be profound. Understanding how you're wired and how your family, friends, colleagues, and comrades are wired can breathe a lot of space into otherwise challenging moments.

"I am large, I contain multitudes."

—Walt Whitman, poet

In their book, *Denying to the Grave: Why We Ignore the Facts That Will Save Us,* Dr. Sara Gorman and Dr. Jack Gorman explore why gaps remain between what is proven in science and what people believe. Their research suggests that people experience genuine pleasure—a rush of dopamine—when processing information that supports their beliefs. Confirmation bias is alluring, but critical thinking can help us stay on our feet. I have been inspired hearing about more and more media literacy programs around the world aimed at helping individuals and communities, beginning with young children, hone the skills needed to recognize misinformation and disinformation, apply self-reflection and personal insight, and contribute toward media justice. An ability to be discerning and to know how to soundly analyze information that is presented to us is immensely important in today's global, political climate. As journalist Bill Moyers said, "Seminary was where I got my questions answered and life is where I got my answers questioned."

Consider the three tenets that, after decades of struggle and revision, musician Lou Reed and artist Laurie Anderson ultimately came to live by: 1. Don't be afraid of anyone. 2. Get a really good bullshit detector. 3. Be really, really tender. This is quite an art, balancing discernment with tenderness. They were not alone in seeing the merit.

"Let us temper our criticism with kindness. None of us comes fully equipped."

—Carl Sagan, astrophysicist and author

SEVEN

Less Depletion, More Stamina

I was so grateful to be lying there amid the quiet of the office, familiar sounds, and soft sheets. And I was so, so tired. I chatted with my gifted acupuncturist before the needles fully took effect and asked if anything could be done to replicate, throughout the day, the feeling that can come from the serotonin coursing through one's system after a high-intensity workout. He finished placing a needle, paused for a second, and said definitively, "Cocaine." While I have not gone that route, I've certainly explored a lot of options to help me outswim what feels like a slow tide pulling me out to a vast body of permanent fatigue.

Standing by a neighborhood pool, talking with a friend, I asked if she ever felt tired. She exhaled and said pointedly, "I have so much less capacity now. For everything." And of course, the sensation of being completely depleted, drained—running on empty—is not exclusive to the older set. My kids are tired, their friends are tired, the kids I work with are tired. And not just tired like on-the-way-home-from-football-practice tired, but *tired*. Of dealing. Exhausted. Flat out. Professionally, this territory of diminished capacity is one of the common denominators in every single field in which I work. It's not just that you're tired. It's truly that sense of, "I can't deal." And the more depleted we become, the more impossible it seems that we should be able to muster the strength to overcome it.

Deep fatigue catches up with folks professionally in countless ways, including inattention to detail, procrastination, missed deadlines, and inferior quality of care. In a discussion at a large conference where I was urging colleagues to not get used to being tired and to not collude with each other being tired, I was sharing how, in my experience, there can be an unspoken ethic that to show how hard you're working you must be somewhat downtrodden. An attendee struck a familiar note and sent a ripple of laughter throughout the room when he said, "With my coworkers, if it looks like anyone showered and put any time into their appearance that day, we all assume they have a job interview."

There is value to us fostering stamina so we can move through our days with more levity and more confidence that we can tend to whatever may arise. Additionally, when the unexpected arises and requires us to find that gear we're not sure we have, having reserves, having a baseline that isn't collapsed, having some stamina, can make a huge difference in how we fare managing our saturation or keeping overwhelm at bay. Remember, less is more. We don't have to do everything at once. In fact, I don't recommend it—it's not sustainable. But do one thing. Do it for a while. Then add something else. Easy does it. As my weightlifting coach said, "These are small movements, but effective."

Depleted?

Once, while traveling, I stopped at a Chipotle for dinner. The restaurant was totally empty. Before I could say anything as I approached the young man behind the counter, he gestured to the completely empty restaurant and said, with a wistful voice, "Man, I just hope it stays like this alllllll night." And one friend who works swing shifts shared with me, "When I get off work and head home, I pull up to my house slowly and just pray that no lights are on and that no one in my family is awake."

When we have this many people feeling this tired, the consequences are many. We're seeing energy drinks used by younger and younger kids. Caffeine is a widespread addiction, and even when folks I work with can have a good sense of humor about choosing one thing they're addicted to and giving it up for a day, man . . . when it comes to caffeine, folks are unamused.

While explaining concerns about how sleep deficient we have become, and the subsequent dependence on caffeine, Matthew Walker put it bluntly: "Caffeine is now at levels of abuse." Walker explains how caffeine interrupts an important biological process this way: "So after 16 hours of being awake, let's say that you have a cup of coffee, an espresso, and all of a sudden, your brain goes from thinking, I've been awake for 16 hours, I'm tired and sleepy, to then thinking, oh, no, hang on a second. I haven't been awake for 16 hours at all. I've only been awake for maybe just six or seven hours because the caffeine is blocking sleep pressure instruction to the brain." This is because adenosine is a chemical that builds up in our brains and makes us sleepy, providing a natural cue that we need to go to sleep. Without adequate sleep, though, adenosine can build up to the point that it becomes increasingly difficult to function (contributing to feelings of overwhelm). Says Walker, "The problem, however, with caffeine is—or one of the problems—there are many—is that when caffeine is blocking those receptors, the adenosine continues to build up. And it continues, and it continues, so that finally, when your brain gets rid of all of that caffeine out of its system, not only do you go back to that level of sleepiness that you were at several hours ago, you're now hit with that level of sleepiness plus all of the additional sleepiness that's been building up in between. And it's what's called the caffeine crash. So now you have to have two espressos rather than just one. And so goes that medication cycle."

One group I worked with talked about how their workplace had finally arrived by getting a brand new elegant espresso machine that dominated their staff kitchen every morning and early afternoon, and *then*—for total balance—at 5:00 pm each day a cocktail cart came through the hallways, rolling by each person's work station. True story.

My friend who is a public defender describes his intimate relationship with the pot of black tea he brews each morning. He says it helps him push through the anxiety he feels as he's gearing up in the morning: "I dread having to put on the armor of responsibility for other people's lives. Caffeine is my liquid motivation." We can be so accustomed to reaching for shortcuts in one area of our life that we may not even see it crop up in other areas. I was sitting at a basketball tournament, watching basketball, when a fellow parent reached for a five-hour energy shot. To help him *watch basketball*.

Instead of hyper-focusing on caffeine as problematic in and of itself, I'd encourage us to consider—with all the sense of humor we can muster—*if* we are clinging tightly, *why* we are clinging tightly, and if there could be benefit in loosening our grip. Even a bit. Whether you reach for caffeine because despite your best efforts you feel perpetually fatigued, or you appreciate the comfortably numb sensation that washes over you when you consume it—if you are feeling any tension from reading this, I encourage you to experiment with possibly more sustainable options.

There's also decision fatigue, which describes the weakening quality of decisions we make after prolonged decision-making. We don't make good decisions when we're mentally depleted—tapped out from too many decisions or too many trade-offs (that is, when choices under consideration have both positive and negative elements).

"Two eggs, any style? My mind is reeling."

Just like tired muscles, the more we make decisions, the more our self-control and willpower wane, our defenses come down, and our brain looks for shortcuts to keep our options open or avoid risk. When we are vulnerable, our inclination may be to become reckless (favoring short-term gains), defer the decision to someone else, or conserve our energy (not decide at all). It's why judges' rulings may vary, a lot, depending on the time of day. Or why car buyers start choosing default options during purchase negotiations.

Decision fatigue has some impact even when the choice is only "paper or plastic." But what happens when our capacity to make decisions is depleted, yet the stakes of the decisions we face are high? When poverty forces people to constantly make high-stakes decisions—pay the light bill or enroll in the night class, save money taking the bus or pick up a child from daycare on time—the impact of decision fatigue can be devastating. The toll of perpetually prioritizing basic needs and making hard trade-offs—as one often does when resources are limited—can mean that people have less ability to show up the way they want or need to in school, jobs, relationships, community efforts, or caring for their own health.

Social psychologist and author Dr. Roy Baumeister has studied decision fatigue around the world. He coined a term called *ego depletion* to explain the limits to our self-control. When we resist something for too long, he says, our willpower starts to give out. The good news is: We can conserve willpower by avoiding exposure to temptation. But this can be hard when temptation seems to be everywhere. Studies show that on average, most people are actively avoiding some type of desire (food, sleep, leisure, looking at their phone, browsing the Internet) for three to four hours a day. Whether you are deciding what class to take, which errand to run, or whether to order soup or a sandwich, call your parents, or eat dessert—it's all contributing to your decision fatigue. And it's not easy to tell when you are maxed out. As journalist and author John Tierney explains, "Ego depletion manifests itself not as one feeling but rather as a propensity to experience everything more intensely. When the brain's regulatory powers weaken, frustrations seem more irritating than usual. Impulses to eat, drink, spend, and say stupid things feel more powerful."

I remember walking through a city with a fifteen-year-old who had just gone through his first break-up. We'd been talking about the copious navigation required to deal with his ex-boyfriend, their friendship group, and his family. While discussing both loose ends that needed tending to and where to get a bite to eat, he stopped midway through an intersection and said, "I'm having a difficult time making decisions."

It's no wonder so many of us are totally tapped out. When our capacity is diminished, and we are overwhelmed, it can feel as if we're running a race to keep up with the machine. And when we're too tired to keep running, life picks us up and takes us, but we're not even touching the ground nor necessarily going in a direction that is any good for us.

Practice building stamina

Being able to sustain ourselves for the long haul requires us to nurture a *deep* well of reserves. In strategizing how to pace oneself in life and to increase one's stamina on any given day, focusing on what's within one's individual control can be especially helpful.

There is a lot of research available to us, ranging from lessons to be learned from the science of willpower to sports physiology. We have many, many options. Regardless of what one chooses, it will take some willingness to commit. We need to give ourselves enough space to work with, without casting opinions about where we are. Once when my daughter was exasperated in the kitchen she said, "I don't feel any better after this health kick I've been doing!" Her sister looked at her in low-grade disbelief and replied with little to no empathy, "It's been a day and a half!" "No," her sister snapped back, "it's been *three!*"

Simplify

One of the ways we can pace ourselves better is by creating conditions to skillfully reduce the volume of decisions we make daily. Shopping for meals ahead of time, scheduling workouts with friends, planning our wardrobe for the week . . . we've all been encouraged to do these things to save *time*, but these habits will also minimize the choices we have to make each day. When we streamline, simplify, and plan ahead, we reduce our daily decision-load, improve our capacity for sound decision-making, and bank some willpower for when we really need it. Start small. Less is more. Pack your bag for the next day, and schedule time to tend to one or two things you've been avoiding. Fill your water bottles first thing each morning. Start with whatever you can wrap your mind around.

It's a tender balance, yes? My daughters tease me relentlessly for the number of times they'll ask me about plans for something happening a few hours in the future, and all I can say is, "That's so far away. We'll figure it out later." You know those days or times in your life when you're truly moment to moment? Mayyyyyybe hour by hour? I find planning to be precarious by nature. We want to schedule our time to ease the noise and chaos in our heads, while also allowing the flexibility to yield to life, such that when things arise we're not totally thrown off our game.

Routine is helpful. Many trauma survivors find it comforting to return to their routine or create a new routine as soon as they can in the aftermath—a practice that is valuable even when mitigating overwhelm on a non-acute scale. Take one step at a time toward solidifying constructive routines for yourself. Reduce your clutter, your possessions, your commitments, and your expectations for perfection . . . and you'll have fewer decisions to make, more spaciousness, and more stamina.

"In order to seek one's own direction, one must simplify the mechanics of ordinary, everyday life."

—Plato, philosopher

Connect your mind and body

I have trained in boxing and remain fascinated by the nuanced art of being responsive without being reactive, and anticipating but not bracing. This requires fluidity, nimbleness, and an unwavering dedication to focus. Of course, the theory of reaction and response is also one we study in relation to the brain. The impulse of *reaction* tends to mimic the animal brain and is a fight-or-flight action, while a *response* tends to be a more expansive, thoughtful activity. Generally, we want to practice being able to *respond* to our environment, rather than defensively reacting.

Peter Berg, actor and filmmaker, shared, "I'm fifty-two years old. And I absolutely love to spar. I'm careful about how I do it. I don't get in there with young guys that are going to knock me out. But the contact and the focus and the energy I get from sparring gives me energy to make movies, energy to be a dad, energy to be a friend, and, you know, makes me feel, probably, a lot younger and behave a lot younger than I am. [People say to me] how can you do it? And I always ask people, how can you *not* do it? You know, if you're a fifty-year-old guy and you're sitting around the house feeling sorry for yourself, get up and move your body and see what it does to your life and to your mind and to your happiness and to your energy levels. I get all that from boxing."

"I can't even begin to work out until I
find the right news to infuriate me."

Even in the realm of political organizing, connecting one's mind and body has been used as an actual strategy both to help folks sustain and to do so effectively. Human rights activist and author Cleve Jones was an intern in the office of politician and pioneer gay-rights leader Harvey Milk, who was known for leading thousands of comrades on long marches through the streets of San Francisco in the 1970s. According to Jones, Milk led the marches not only to draw attention to their cause but also to tire the activists out enough so they could effectively convey their message without becoming violent.

For Warmth

I hold my face in my two hands.
No, I am not crying.
I hold my face in my two hands
to keep the loneliness warm—
two hands protecting,
two hands nourishing,
two hands preventing
my soul from leaving me
in anger.

—Thich Nhat Hanh

I have been particularly drawn to the growing field of psychobiology and have found benefit in learning what contributes to the impressive performance of endurance athletes—and how we can apply that to our everyday lives. Historically, it was believed that an athlete's endurance was primarily limited by muscle fatigue due to lack of oxygen and excess production of lactic acid. But new science indicates that endurance athletes usually stop performing well before their muscles give out. They stop because of *perception of effort*—the maximum level of effort they *think* they can tolerate—proving that fatigue is more of a mental phenomenon than a physical one.

As journalist and author Matt Fitzgerald writes, "What endurance athletes must endure above all is not *actual* effort but *perception* of effort. One cannot improve as an endurance athlete except by changing one's relationship with perception of effort." Perceived effort is what causes a Tour de France cyclist to fade on their last mountain climb or a marathon runner to surge forward in the last mile. Clinical exercise physiologist Dr. Samuele Marcora explains, "Perception of effort reflects 'central motor command,' the brain activity necessary to voluntarily activate the muscles. Decisions about pacing or quitting during endurance competitions are made by the conscious brain, and these decisions are primarily based on the conscious feeling of how hard, heavy, and strenuous exercise is." He points out, though, that this isn't just a matter of willpower. Physical capacity and mental fatigue play a role as well, but "the muscles can only perform to the degree that the mind is able to cope."

So how can we apply the notion of perceived effort to our everyday ability to sustain, even for something as mundane as our to-do list?

- Be grateful for what your body and mind allow you to do. For the opportunities they provide. Give thanks through working, resting, eating well, and hydrating a lot.
- When possible, spend time doing those things you feel most passionate about and least neurotic about.
- Practice mindfulness: Use meditation, positive self-talk, goal setting, and imagery. And when all else fails, have a sense of humor and smile. One of my mentors assured me that if I can't actually smile, it can be helpful to just start by slightly turning up the corners of my mouth.

I have never considered myself an endurance athlete. Ever. But during a 122-kilometer bike ride from Vancouver, Canada, to Whistler, I discovered just how useful it can be to work on shifting one's perception of the situation when changing the situation itself isn't a viable option. I agreed to the ride in the first place as an excuse to spend time with friends (all badass athletes, unlike myself) and because I thought it would provide good reflection time. Throughout the ride, I kept a sense of humor, but it especially paid off and saved me from losing steam altogether during one particularly long, slow ascent. As is often the case during races, photographers were stationed along the route, and I saw one as I lifted my head to gauge how much longer I'd be climbing a grueling hill. He had been squatting down reviewing his previous shots when he must have sensed me coming and looked up to assess the situation. Then he dropped his eyes, shook his head, packed his gear, and jumped on his moped. No photo was taken. Being able to laugh to myself helped subsequent miles feel less exhausting.

One of my role models when it comes to applying perception of effort to how to sustain in everyday life is Maria Toorpakai. She grew up in Waziristan, Pakistan, home to the Taliban—and where some believe that women's sports are un-Islamic and where girls are often not allowed to go to school. Supported by incredible parents, at four years old she began to pass as a boy to try to maintain some freedom. Her parents helped her train in weightlifting and squash, the second biggest sport in Pakistan. As a teenager, Maria was ranked third in the world. Over time, her success caught the attention of the Taliban, and she began receiving death threats. As a matter of necessity, she stopped going outside and trained in her room—for more than three years. "All I could think of was playing squash. I worked very hard and trained for almost ten hours every day. Squash is very close to my heart, my soul. It became a matter of survival for me," she said. For four years she sent up to ninety emails a day to squash academies, organizations, and universities seeking help from outside of Pakistan. Ultimately, she was invited to attend a squash academy in Canada.

I spoke with Maria in late 2017, and it is hard to describe the clarity of her focus and her commitment to putting one foot in front of the other, every single day. She runs a foundation aimed at helping children, she trains daily, and she lives separated from her entire family and homeland. She shared, "I try to see everything that happens as positively as I can and as some kind of a lesson. We should always look for beautiful things in our lives. It is more fun for me in life to view things as a challenge, even when I'm scared. I have a very strong faith and I believe there must be some purpose out there. I try to be focused on where I think I can help others the most. For me, squash makes me very happy. I do that every day and I try to learn something new every day. In life. It doesn't matter how little it is. But, for me, then I know I'm still progressing. I am aware that life has no guarantees. Why waste the present you have in your hands?"

Appreciate nature

Being in nature is another option that has widespread benefits toward helping us increase our energy and ability to endure for the long haul. Poet and essayist Ralph Waldo Emerson reminds us to "Live in the sunshine, swim the sea, drink the wild air." I couldn't contain the smile that came over my face when on a crowded plane I saw a fellow passenger coming down the aisle with a shirt that said, "Nature. Cheaper than therapy."

"The majestic way they climb higher and higher until they seem to kiss the sky reminds me of the huge pile of work I have waiting for me when I get back."

Earlier, we discussed the value of being in nature as it relates to regulating one's nervous system, allowing one to be more present. But again I want to reinforce that you don't have to hike for miles or kayak open water to gain the benefits of being outside. This can simply be about taking a five-minute break from classes, work, or sitting at someone's bedside. Instead of walking the hallways on one's phone or engaging in conversations that are (at times) beneath us, step outside and look up at the sky. An investment of only a few minutes can efficiently help build our stamina. I know teachers who move as many classes as they can outside and colleagues who take almost all their small meetings as walking meetings outside.

"Nature can be sanity inducing."

—Bruce Springsteen

Outdoor retailer REI went all-in touting the benefits of being in nature with their #OptOutside campaign, which started when they made the bold decision to close their stores on the day after Thanksgiving in the U.S., giving staff the day off and encouraging people to explore the outdoors instead of participating in the holiday shopping frenzy. [So smart. Who *isn't* looking for a source of stamina during the holidays?]

More broadly, natural beauty elicits strong feelings of awe. My friend Grace Brown, activist and photographer, had just returned from a summer camp in Maine when she described a moment she hadn't been able to shake. The camp took pre-teens from the different boroughs of New York City and hosted them at a college campus. Grace was struck by watching an eleven-year-old sit down with wonderment in an open space of beautiful, green grass. It was the first time she had sat down in grass. Ever.

Stanford researcher Dr. Melanie Rudd conducted a study that concluded that awe—especially when prompted by natural beauty—is stimulating, because it expands people's perception of time and space and prompts them to mentally accommodate the grandeur of what they're experiencing. Many cultures and traditions talk about the interweaving of what is permanent and what is impermanent. The mountains. The sky. The light that follows darkness. Seasons. Reflecting for yourself on what feels most comforting and nourishing is a first step toward deepening your stamina. A mentor from a trauma center shared that for years she cherished time spent visiting the ocean. But there came a time, years into professional and personal overwhelm, when what she craved instead was proximity to a quiet, slow-moving river.

Draw on spirituality and religion

The role that spirituality and religion can play in our ability to sustain is significant and, for some, critical. Whether experienced in private prayer or in a massive congregation, Bryan Stevenson reminds us, "You don't have to have the answers, you just have to have a heart willing to stand in community." That community may be human-, animal-, or wilderness-based, but for some people, great comfort comes from connecting with something larger than ourselves.

My friend Steven Wilbur is the principal of Hope Academy, which is a school dedicated to children in Lebanon who have been neglected or victims of various kinds of abuse, including sex trafficking, drug experimentation, and human organ trafficking. Many things help Steven get through gut-wrenching days. His Christian faith is of paramount importance. Also, eating fatteh any chance he gets. He notes:

> "I play music for hours—it really helps me to focus on something completely different, like Miles Davis. I think imagination and creating is helpful; it's a positive action. Of course, exercise helps . . . when I do it. I think sleep is helpful, but I can't say I do it. For me, I see this work as being of God. I don't believe I could do what I'm doing without God's help. It might be too much. And just having that narrative—that there's a loving God who loved humanity as much as he did, that he made sacrifice after sacrifice. I think a lot about how Jesus was humble but confident, and a lot of what he did was radical for the time. I am doing a lot of praying and relying on 'I don't have the strength, please give me the strength. I have a lot of inner turmoil, please give me peace today.' And, sometimes, after a particularly hard day, I'll take a long shower and meet a friend for dinner. I'll remind myself that it's over. Everything that happened today is over, and now I'm going to devour some fatteh."

Some talk about spirituality in terms of looking at deep time. When we create an open space in which we are being moved, instead of moving, we can extend time and space. Rest and motion aren't antithetical, after all. In many martial arts, we practice *being*, without tension. Moving meditation. And the relaxation of our body and our mind can do wonders toward giving us strength to endure. This is important. As one resident advisor in a dorm at an Ivy League university told me after a long season of suicide attempts, sexual assaults, and students having crises back home, "The amount of down time I'm needing is more and more, but the problem is, I don't have that time." The recognition that we must reclaim our time from the mundane in order to renew and recenter is an ancient and enduring insight.

Virtually every faith tradition instructs its adherents to reserve time from the demands of the secular world for reflection and appreciation, whether that be observing an annual cycle of holidays, fasting during Ramadan, stopping work on Shabbat, daily prayer and meditation, making a pilgrimage, attending a sweat, reveling in choir practice, or even reciting a verse of scripture. Religious and spiritual practices can be of assistance whether folks are walking to a meeting reciting a prayer or holding one's gold cross necklace in hand during a particularly stressful moment in school. Ancient traditions share these invaluable lessons: Create space internally and cultivate a vast perspective within—over and over again.

Admire art

Then there is art. One of the great gifts of art, it seems, is there is something for everyone. Graffiti art, the opera, sculpture, rap, photography, poetry, architecture, landscaping. The design and craftsmanship of furniture, tools, and instruments. Whether one is appreciating art or creating it, art has the power to transport us. Writer William Faulkner asserted in his Nobel Prize acceptance speech that the role of the writer is "to help man endure by lifting his heart."

I consider observing folks who do a task well akin to watching an artist at work. Whether watching a chef prepare a meal or a teacher capture the attention of an entire classroom, I've come to take notice and give myself a moment to appreciate their craft. I usually find myself quietly saying, "Man, how do they *do* that?!" This happened when my daughter and I were introduced by our friends at the University of Wisconsin to two nuclear physicists. Generous with their time and gracious with their patience in how much we didn't know, they showed us around their lab, explained their research, and fielded our questions. The passion with which they communicated both the content of their work and the way they approach it daily—even to folks who couldn't begin to decipher anything written on the massive white boards encircling the labs—was nothing short of an art form. This is one of the many blessings of art, yes? It doesn't have to make intellectual sense to us to make us feel deeply. Sometimes that feeling alone can nourish us for days, or even years.

Photo by M. Lipsky. Paris, France

For centuries, music has been a proven remedy to help people find a way through. One neuroscientist shared with me how much she gains from syncing with various tempos throughout her day, since the tempos we listen to can affect the tempos in our minds. She has one playlist for waking up, another for walking to work, another for returning home, and another to help her wind down her day.

Hymns and spirituals, passed down for generations, tell stories of pain but also express faith and hope for freedom—freedom from bondage and freedom from sin. And in many traditions, music helps us grieve, for as Aldous Huxley wrote, "After silence, that which comes nearest to expressing the inexpressible is music."

Lin-Manuel Miranda, creator of *Hamilton: An American Musical*, and Oskar Eustis, artistic director of the Public Theater, profoundly illustrate the power of music:

" [Mr. Eustis's] 16-year-old son, Jack, took his own life . . . Mr. Eustis, with his family, faces the kind of soul-searching for which there can be no preparation. How to hold on and move forward at the same time. What it means to be a public figure with a private grief. . . .

An MP3 arrived by email, hours after Jack's death. It came from Lin-Manuel Miranda, a new arrival to the Public fold.

It was a demo recording of "It's Quiet Uptown," the song from "Hamilton" describing Alexander Hamilton, and his wife, Eliza, as they grieve the death of their 19-year-old son, Philip:

> There are moments that the words don't reach
> There is suffering too terrible to name
> You hold your child as tight as you can
> And push away the unimaginable
> The moments when you're in so deep
> It feels easier to just swim down.

"There is nothing you can say," Mr. Miranda recalled thinking. "And yet, I had a song about this. So I wrote to him saying, 'If this is useful, then lean on it, and, if not, delete this email.'"

Mr. Eustis and his wife found it useful. "Every line of 'Quiet Uptown' feels like it's exactly correct to my experience," Mr. Eustis said. "It was the only music we listened to for a long time, and we listened to it every day, and it became a key thing for the two of us." . . .

But Mr. Eustis and Mr. Miranda both recall something else, too: The grieving father's reaction to a line of comic relief that, in the show's libretto, is uttered by Thomas Jefferson immediately after "It's Quiet Uptown": "Can we get back to politics?"

"For me, the beautiful thing about 'Quiet Uptown' is, it serves a ritualistic function—it takes us into the grief, and then it takes us out of it," Mr. Eustis said. "And there's nothing, there's no other ritual that I know of, that can do that for me."

—Michael Paulson, theater reporter for *The New York Times*

"Studies show that people who allow art into their lives can substantially reduce their dependency on selective serotonin reuptake inhibitors."

Laugh

Few things are more reliably healing and transformative than humor. Ethical humor. Not humor at the expense of others nor cynical humor. A sense of humor applied responsibly in your own experience can do wonders toward helping you endure. And then there are comedians and humorists, amusing essayists, who have honed their gift for releasing tension and broadening our perspective through their art. Reimagining a vignette through the lens of humorists Jenny Lawson or David Rakoff can turn the mundane to brilliant. The more humor—with a sprinkle of humility—you can bring into your life the better.

"I developed my sense of humor as a defense mechanism and turned it into a lethal offensive weapon."

Engage with community

Finding our people and avoiding isolation can also help us fortify our stamina. Whether in very large lifesaving ways or seemingly small dignity-preserving ways, reaching out through what may otherwise be isolating moments in our days or seemingly never-ending hard times can be powerful. As one attorney shared, "The power of knowing that terrible, or even just unhappy, experiences are shared by others is, for me anyway, an incredible palliative. We're all in this together and I am not alone in my grief. And I'll likely survive because other humans have."

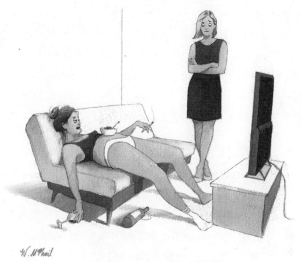

"I'm between reasons right now."

I am fascinated by the massive, sprawling teams of emergency-response volunteers in Iceland. The way they mobilize and care for their communities (including countless tourists) is breathtaking. The network is known as Slysavarnafélagið Landsbjörg, or, in English, the Icelandic Association for Search and Rescue—ICE-SAR. As reporter Nick Paumgarten describes, "Calamity is commonplace in Iceland, and rescue is sanctified." He reports:

"Iceland, with a population of little more than three hundred thousand, is the only NATO country with no standing Army. It has police, and a coast guard, but these, like the citizens they are paid to protect, are spread thin, so come accident or disaster, disappearance or storm, the citizens, for the most part, have always had to fend for themselves. Landsbjörg has evolved into a regimented volunteer system that serves as a peerless kind of national-emergency militia. It is not a government program, and so represents a tithing of manpower. There are close to ten thousand members in all, with four thousand of them on 'callout' duty, on ninety-seven teams. Pretty much every town has a team. They are well trained and well equipped, self-funded and self-organizing, and enjoy a near-mythical reputation among their countrymen, who, though often agnostic regarding the existence of elves and gnomes, are generally not inclined toward reverence or exaggeration. 'People think of the rescue teams as the Guardians of the Galaxy,' a mountain guide told me. 'They forget these are normal people.'"

Landsbjörg's search and rescue units are so renowned they've been called in to assist with disasters worldwide. But we don't need to participate in an epic tradition to extend ourselves in community. One early morning, while out for a run in a very industrial area in Los Angeles, I passed a bus stop. There were several folks standing, waiting for the bus, and one gentleman sleeping on the bench, bundled up, his few possessions in a ripped plastic bag under him. I watched as a city employee, obviously charged with upkeep of this stop, cleaned everything she could around the shelter. When it came time to clean that bench, she slowed down and took great care to not disturb the sleeping man. She was meticulous in both getting her job done and in caring for someone she may have never seen before. A quiet, tender gesture amid the rush of the morning commute.

Continuing to dismantle barriers that otherwise isolate us, even when backed by systemic power, can have profound influence. During a time in the U.S. when the three largest mental health centers are prisons, I particularly appreciated hearing about the generosity of District Court Judge Lou Olivera. As a consequence for recurrent transgressions, Judge Olivera sentenced a veteran to one night in jail. But recognizing that that one night in a cell could have extreme consequences to the man, who was suffering from PTSD, the judge made arrangements to stay in the cell with him. They spent the night talking through their shared experiences and strategizing how the man could turn his life around. Imagine the impact that one night may have had . . . on both men, really.

"The world is not comprehensible, but it is embraceable: through the embracing of one of its beings."

—Martin Buber, philosopher and political activist

There is a park I spend time in whenever I can. It's said to be in the most diverse zip code in the United States; those who frequent this park represent many different cultures, speak different languages, and practice different customs. And on some days, special days, moments transpire that could not be planned or orchestrated and that leave us all feeling blessed. Sometimes as runners are doing their sprints; grandparents are pushing baby strollers; artists are out with easels; and groups of old friends in pairs and trios are walking their familiar, beaten path— sometimes an eagle (or two) will fly overhead. And time slows down. Every time. Everyone comes together, one way or another. Sprinters slow their pace and raise their gaze, grandparents kneel to help grandchildren see, artists put down their brushes to look, and the chatter of old friends tapers to a hush as everyone's attention turns to the sky. It's rare that anyone says anything, but we all pause, watch, and take it in. In community. Writer Robert Brault shared, "Enjoy the little things in life because one day you'll look back and realize they were the big things."

Our community includes folks we have never met but also those known folks we turn to in times of need: our go-to people. These people may change as we age and move and evolve, but knowing when to ask for help and being willing to follow through can be truly lifesaving. Given what we know intuitively about loneliness, combined with compelling research around the wide-scale and varied impacts of being isolated, we would be wise to prioritize connecting with others. Sometimes those we find comfort in are trainers at the gym, sometimes they're childhood friends. Sometimes the voice you need to hear is the host of your favorite podcast or the lead singer of your all-time favorite song. We have options.

My daughter cracked up during a conversation about community with one of her basketball coaches, whom she greatly admires. Coach ShaKiana Edwards-Teasley is older than my daughter, but not, you know, too old. She is very hip, hugely cool, incredibly accomplished in the states and abroad, the same combination mixed race as my girls, and the daughter of an NBA player. So here is this badass athlete, towering above my daughter at 6'1", and I asked what she did when she felt in over her head. Without missing a beat, she said, "I call my mom. Like, a lot. All the time."

One of the most meaningful ways we can contribute to community is to take an intentional pause when bearing witness to anything hard. As teachers and mentors have reminded me, we are all connected, and the ritual of pausing can be a powerful bridge. Whether the person directly in front of us is struggling or tragedy has shaken the world, it is meaningful to honor the pain of others by holding them authentically in our thoughts and hearts. There will be times when tending to suffering requires our physical presence through advocating or volunteering. There will be times when it takes the form of calling someone in government, writing to those who may hold power, making a donation, or preparing a meal. There will be times when prayer and meditation or lighting a symbolic candle are appropriate. And while of course this does not remedy everything—not even close—tending to the suffering of others in whatever way we can is important to our humanity—and our liberation. Let us aspire to not allow overwhelm in the midst of suffering to leave us feeling powerless. There is always something we can do.

One of the first times I remember recognizing the power of pausing to acknowledge another was the day after my mother's death. While I don't remember much about the days surrounding her passing, the details I do recall remain incredibly vivid. My friend took me home with her, so I could get out of my house for a bit. We were thirteen at the time, and she had a seventeen-year-old brother. I knew him, and he was always nice, but he was older and immeasurably cooler and I never felt remotely worthy of attention from him or his crew. That afternoon, still totally in shock, I descended the stairs with her to the basement where I could hear the antics of her brother and his friends who were wrestling in a completely chaotic and wild pack. As we entered the room, her brother caught sight of me and said, "Wait, wait, stop!" to his friends in a distinct and unwavering tone. He shook them off and rushed toward me, enveloping me in his huge frame. It was a long hug, and as I recall he uttered maybe only three or four words. That was it. But, honestly—that was everything. I will never forget it.

EIGHT

When to Step Away

There is a Hasidic story of a respected rabbi who taught his disciples to memorize and contemplate teachings and place the prayers and holy words on their heart. A day came when one of the disciples asked the rabbi why he always said "on your heart" and not "in your heart," and the rabbi replied, "Only time and grace can put the essence of these stories in your heart. Here we recite and learn them and put them on our hearts hoping that someday, when our heart breaks, they will fall in."

Once we deepen our insight and awareness into how our lives are currently going, if the way we're spending our time is edifying or eroding, we have a final set of considerations to evaluate. A central tenet of our ability to sustain is being able to discern when to approach, when to maintain, and when to call it a wrap.

This ranges from the countless small decisions that make up our waking hours to the major choices that punctuate our life. Sometimes, one of the most self-preserving choices we can make is when we're done—even for the day. I think frequently about my friend's two-year-old nephew who midway through dinner stopped eating, put his sweet little hands down on the table, and said resolutely, "I am done being awake."

Make informed choices

Whether we are assessing the merit of staying in a particular school, shifting friend groups, pursuing an internship, continuing a certain level of caregiving, remaining employed, dedicating ourselves to a cause, or even speaking some words that are right on the tip of our tongues, the privileges and responsibilities we have to make informed choices each step of the way cannot be understated. As we've pointed out, there are endless moments in our days and junctures in our lives when we have options. We may have lots of options, or we may have only a few. But especially when the options are fewer, we want to remember what we do have control over. And one of those things is *if* and *how much* to be involved, connected, or engaged.

"It's too late, Roger—they've seen us."

If it's a small break you need to keep on keeping on, give yourself some time and space to Just. Do. Nothing. Step out for a minute.

The benefit of this was revealed to me during a family reunion. You may be able to relate to this. Lots of people around, complex dynamics at play. Surely, you've been there? So, in this particular moment, I was trying to get my partner's attention to help both tend to the adult situation at hand and help wrangle the many children running around at our feet. He was uncharacteristically not picking up on my, "Hey, there, wanna join me over here?" look. When I finally intercepted his thoughts and he recognized my look of, "What the ?!?!" he maintained eye contact with me and slowly brought his right hand up to his mouth as if holding something. Then I heard him softly make the very deliberate and unmistakable sound of inhaling and slowly exhaling that happens when using a regulator while scuba diving. I knew then how far away he was.

There is a practice in scuba diving that if someone you're diving with is running out of air in their tank, you pass your regulator back and forth: buddy breathing. So, there we were, far from anywhere you could scuba dive, and amid all the chaos around us, he extends his imagined regulator out to me offering a breath. Although tempted, I declined. After a few more moments, he resurfaced and began to tend to the needs at hand.

Our capitalist society and cultural pressures that praise staying in motion to the nth degree may steer you otherwise, but drawing parameters and reigning it in can be a self-respecting move. I work with folks in field after field where the frenetic nature of the culture (and our own martyrdom) can get so extreme it's as if folks working for *this* cause get to the point of looking at folks serving *that* cause, or folks in *this* department look at folks in *that* department, and say, "*Your* people take time to go pee during the day? Interesting. *We* get much more done going the dehydration route. We're so much more productive when we don't stop and pee during the day."

Essayist Tim Kreider calls us out for buying into the hysteria that *busy* equals *valuable*, and he advocates taking a step back. "Idleness is not just a vacation, an indulgence or a vice; it is as indispensable to the brain as vitamin D is to the body," he says. "The space and quiet that idleness provides is a necessary condition for standing back from life and seeing it whole, for making unexpected connections and waiting for the wild summer lightning strikes of inspiration—it is, paradoxically, necessary to getting any work done." Say "no" to something. Clear your plate a bit. Then consider setting stricter parameters about where you allocate your time going forward. Or, maybe you need a *real* separation from that which is causing you pain.

Many of us might have deep, long passed-down meaning associated with staying. Staying can mean we are loyal, dedicated, steadfast, faithful, reliable, or strong. Filmmaker Joe Berlinger, when talking about the responsibility he felt in making the documentary *Paradise Lost*, shared,

"My first kid was born while we were editing this film and I would be sitting at the editing bay, looking at the most horrific autopsy photos and crime scene footage. I would go home at night after having these images emblazoned on [my] brain and I would drop the door of the crib and pick up my new infant, who had just arrived a few months ago, and holding my child and thinking about these eight-year-olds and thinking about the gross autopsy footage that I had looked at . . . Every hallmark that my child would go through—kindergarten, middle school, high school—I'd think, 'My God, these guys are still rotting in prison.' I just felt we had a moral obligation to keep telling the story."

Our inclination to remain engaged could spring from religious upbringing to internalized oppression or expectations from our culture or families to a set of beliefs around what it means to be successful or simply a "good" person. Of course, staying isn't always an expression of our best values. Staying can also reflect stubbornness, inertia, inflexibility, or simple force of habit. Let's remember, impermanence can be a gift. There is opportunity where the old leaf makes way for a new bud to flourish.

> "When we understand the truth of impermanence and find our composure in it, there we find ourselves in Nirvana."
>
> —Suzuki Roshi, Zen priest

I have worked in early childhood education as long as I've done trauma work, and I was the founder and director of a Spanish language preschool. For more than a decade our curriculum was taught within a framework of social and environmental justice, and I often reflect on the many lessons all those preschoolers and I learned together over the years. One of the lessons was about "walk away power"—common lexicon in our home to this day. Given my work in child abuse and neglect, I felt it important to provide these two- to five-year-olds strategies in how to try to remove themselves from situations where they felt unsettled or unsafe. Skilled self-defense and safety awareness instructors came each year to role-play with the children, practicing their walk away power. Someone says something unkind to you or to someone you're with, and you try to ask them to stop and they don't? Use your walk away power! That one relative sits too close to you on the couch? Use your walk away power! You have hair that it seems like everyone feels entitled to touch even after you use your words the best you can? Use your walk away power!

My daughters' lives have not gotten less complicated since those days, but we still remind them that walking away, even if it's only in your mind, remains an option. And of course, as adults, there's no shortage of opportunities to practice this.

Question whether and how to remain

Actively questioning if remaining at all and *how* we remain are essential to our own well-being and, of course, to those we're aspiring to help. Too often we gain clarity only after a crisis or when we've hit an all-time low. A colleague once shared a poignant moment that happened when her child unknowingly gave her an opportunity to consider 1. if the cause she was involved in was where she actually wanted to be, and 2. if she *did* stay, how much reframing might be required for her to believe she was making a difference. She had dedicated her life to gun violence prevention and worked incredibly hard to do what she could, to great personal sacrifice. That morning, before she came to the retreat, her young son had seen the Breaking News feed come across their television about a mass shooting. "Mommy," he said. "You failed at your job."

Through daily reflection on "to what benefit?" we can make decisions about if, and how, we spend our time as proactively as we possibly can.

"They tried to bury us. They didn't know we were seeds."

—Dinos Christianopoulos, poet

I imagine we can all relate to that very hard place of having changed or evolved or just even shifted slightly in who we are and how we go about being ourselves. Sometimes shifts are met with support and understanding, but often folks are attached to who we *were*, which is often in service to their needs.

Someone who has grown up in a family of middle-class, assimilated, American parents, for example, is already an inheritor of the Great American tradition of cutting ties with the old world in order to "actualize" your own self. Registering the costs may be less of a priority because, in many cases, the costs have been paid by previous generations. On some level, your family of origin understands breaking from a situation that doesn't help reach your goals, because the old traditions, land, or obligations were already forfeited by the previous generation. For people involved in a family still tied to its traditions—land, language, obligations, myth, and superstition—to make that leap into one's own actualization is a fraught and costly one, often alienating and isolating, not fundamentally liberating. The payoff is frequently not what we think and, instead, results in further overwhelm—often living beyond our means financially, emotionally, physically, and/or environmentally. The sacrifices that come with cultural assimilation, in this case, may be easier to calculate.

Some launch away from their homeland and loved ones because it's what is expected of them by the dominant culture, others to survive in globalized capitalism, and still others because their lives depend upon it.

> "My mother was the first person in her family to graduate from college. I graduated only a few years after her, and my mom's family was still ambivalent about it. My mom was a grown woman with five kids when she graduated, they were sure she was set in her ways. But for my generation, they were worried. They wanted people to succeed, but they were afraid that we would move into different circles, that we would forget 'where we came from,' that we would leave them, the things they valued and the very things that had sustained us in life such that we could go to school and graduate.
>
> When I graduated from college, one of my aunts said to me, 'I brought your great-grandfather's coin collection to give you for your graduation.' I was touched, and a little confused. My great-grandfather was a sharecropper with no money. I

never knew he had a coin collection. My aunt handed me a small, very worn coin purse with a metal clasp. The leather was brittle, and there were several seams where the leather had been mended over the years. Inside was one nickel. I looked up at my aunt, and the look in her face was so fierce. So torn. She said. 'Children never went hungry and old folks were never left alone. You're no better than anybody else, so don't you forget what you came from.'

That was it. And she was right. That education and the path I took from it set me apart from them. I love them, but I was different and was not truly in orbit with them any longer.

She knew this. Huck Finn's dad knew this. In America, we only tell the story of the families that seek out this rupture. Who tell their kids, 'Leave us behind and grab your brass ring.' But this was not my experience. It was a different choice I was making. "

—Connie Burk

Another factor we may consider in when to step away is if we feel we can no longer be, truly, who we want to be given the projections or constraints on us. A young college student described the disappointment he experienced when he returned home, eager to share with his friends after traveling internationally doing service projects. He said, "Honestly, I feel like no one even cared. No one even wanted to really hear about it. Not only that but I'll call my friends from back home and I genuinely feel like they don't want to talk with me anymore because I won't make fun of people or punk people out like we used to."

The importance of assessing one's capacity at any given time and honoring oneself and one's ability was impressed upon me when I was asked to work with a university and the surrounding community in 2017. At an annual dinner my hosts organized, I had the joy of getting to talk with some elders about their time in the civil rights movement and their perception of the current state of affairs in the U.S. One of the gentlemen acknowledged the price we pay when we show up and try—on any level—to help: "If you're going to really be a part of creating change it's gonna cost ya. If it's not costing you, you're not in the movement."

*"Thanks for walking a mile in my shoe
but it's beginning to hurt now."*

And sometimes choosing whether and how to remain is especially difficult in situations we didn't choose for ourselves in the first place. Robin Brulé has faced painful choices that she never thought possible. Her elderly mother and her mother's friend were murdered in their home. The women were drinking coffee and reading the daily newspaper when three assailants broke into the house and killed them. I have witnessed Robin and her family move through the aftermath of this horror, and I was in awe as Robin shared each deliberate decision she made to try to preserve what felt like a precarious hold on her sanity.

When the families were asked to appear at the first sentencing hearing, Robin sought ways to manage her circumstances—amid so many factors beyond her individual control. She chose to attend and speak at the trial, so the record would be complete, and her children would not be burdened with recounting events during parole hearings years later. She carefully chose the words she used to describe her mother with dignity, so her mother would not live on in the memory of the court as a victim. She chose to limit her time in the courtroom, to remain only as long as necessary to support her brother and sister. She chose where to sit and where to look so as not to cast eyes on one of the men who took her mother's life. And she chose to be accompanied by a therapy dog. And, in that, she allowed herself to be taken care of in ways she didn't know she would need.

During the opening statement, the prosecutor addressed the court and spared no detail in sharing exactly how the murders had unfolded. Overcome at one point, Robin fell down, got up, and ran to the family respite room with the dog at her heels. On her knees, head in her hands, the dog gently placed his head on her back. He kept it resting there as a torrent of tears were shed, until Robin was ready to return to court. After the hearing, Robin recounted, "I learned something about myself. Through all of this and the overwhelm of being in that courtroom and seeing my mother's murderer and hearing those details . . . I realized I cannot allow myself to go to the places in my mind it would otherwise take me . . . I cannot allow myself to go there. The rage I felt was like venom in me, and I thought about what it was doing inside of me . . . and what it was doing to me . . . and that harm is not something I want for myself."

Robin chose to find agency in wretched circumstances foisted upon her. We always have choices.

"Look deeply within, even if the way you get there is through a crisis."

—Thich Nhat Hanh

Conclusion

My daughter was ten, we think, when a tumor started growing in her bone. It was benign. Still it grew and grew. After three years of appointments to our local children's hospital and hawk-like watching, doctors concluded that a very large mass should be removed from her leg. Surgery was long but went well, and the surgeon was truly a saint, as was the nurse who had cared for us throughout. Her father and I literally paced back and forth in the hospital room (so cliché) where we'd get to see her as soon as they'd allow us to after the procedure. She held up well, and a few hours later when the heavy narcotics given during surgery had worn off, the attending doctor stopped by during rounds. Confounded that she'd not taken any pain meds after surgery, he said he'd never seen anyone not need them. I said out loud to my daughter, "Hey, babe, nice pain threshold!" The doctor spun around and glared at me. Sternly, he reprimanded, "Or she is *very* brave and *very* skilled with her ability to manage her pain with her focus."

We've gotten some good mileage out of that moment to be sure, but it has remained with me as I consider what may be helpful as we navigate our own individual and collective sense of overwhelm. Surely there is—for each of us—what we're born with, including all the light and all the shadows. And then there's our training. It is never too late to start a new practice, merging the reality of insight about who you are—with an understanding of all you've got going on—with awareness of the choices you can make to help you sustain for the long haul. Do *something*. Every day.

One of my favorite remedies for overwhelm is backpacking. Though it's not something I do every day, there are rhythms from it that I carry with me always. One of the customs I love most about backpacking is the intuitive yielding that happens on the trail. On trails with elevation, ascending hikers always have the right of way. Hikers coming downhill step aside and yield, allowing uphill hikers to pass safely. This is particularly important, of course, when hikers are carrying heavy backpacks and when the trail is sketchy.

This custom is typically conducted in silence—or maybe with a knowing nod—but if you do hear exchanges they're almost always that of encouragement: "It's worth it" or "You're almost there" or "Not too much farther" or even just "Come on up, we'll wait." Almost inevitably, throughout one's hike, there are numerous such moments of yielding, grace, and gratitude.

Also, trail etiquette is indifferent to social rank or status. Hikers may be old or young, experienced (or not), famous (or not), with gear that's fancy or frayed. But everyone observes the custom, honoring the effort of uphill travelers who may be breathing hard, with aching body parts, possibly wondering why, yet again, they chose to spend their time this way. But in all the years I've gone backpacking, I've never seen anyone be anything less than patient, understanding, empathetic, and kind during the seconds it takes to yield or proceed.

Author and humanitarian Elie Wiesel said, "For me, every hour is grace." As we continue on, individually and collectively, may we all find those moments—big and small—when we yield and proceed, with grace and determination, with discernment about how we can refrain from causing harm, with clarity about how we can contribute wisely, and with some ability to be grateful—for something—along the way.

NOTES

Quotes from interviews may have been edited and condensed for clarity.

PAGE VII: Desmond Tutu, public lecture, Seattle, Washington.

PAGE XV: Albert Camus, *The Rebel: An Essay on Man in Revolt,* trans. Anthony Bower (New York: Vintage Books, 1956).

INTRODUCTION

PAGE 3: Toni Morrison, "No Place for Self-Pity, No Room for Fear," *Nation,* March 23, 2015, https://www.thenation.com/article/no-place-self-pity-no-room-fear/.

PAGE 4: Audre Lord, *A Burst of Light* (Ithaca, NY: Firebrand, 1988), quoted in Aisha Harris, "A History of Self-Care," CultureBox, *Slate,* April 5, 2017, http://www.slate.com/articles/arts/culturebox/2017/04/the_history_of_self_care.html.

PAGE 5: Terry Tempest Williams, *The Open Space of Democracy* (Eugene, OR: Wipf & Stock, 2004), 83.

PAGE 7: Saint Augustine, *Confessions,* Book 10, c. 397, quoted in Linda J.T., *Oceans of Wisdom* (Bloomington, IN: Balboa Press, 2013), 95.

PAGE 7: Rick Hanson, "Relax, You're Going to Be Criticized," *Dr. Rick Hanson* (blog), accessed 02/06/18, http://www.rickhanson.net/relax-youre-going-to-be-criticized/.

PAGE 8: Joan Didion, "On Self-Respect: Joan Didion's 1961 Essay from the Pages of *Vogue,*" *Vogue,* October 22, 2014, https://www.vogue.com/article/joan-didion-self-respect-essay-1961.

PAGE 9: Malcolm Gladwell, "Mr. Hollowell Didn't Like That," *Revisionist History,* podcast, season 2, episode 8, August 2, 2017, http://revisionist history.com/episodes/18-mr-hollowell-didnt-like-that. Transcript available at https://blog.simonsays.ai/mr-hollowell-didnt-like-that-with-malcolm-gladwell-s2-e8-revisionist-history-podcast-7fe252e81f32.

PAGE 9: "Dolores Huerta Biography," Biography.com, accessed 02/06/18, https://www.biography.com/people/dolores-huerta-188850.

PAGE 11: James Baldwin, *Nobody Knows My Name: More Notes of a Native Son* (New York: Dial Press, 1961), 154.

PAGE 12: Hafiz, *The Gift: Poems by Hafiz, the Great Sufi Master*, trans. Daniel Ladinsky (New York: Penguin Books, 1999), 328.

PAGE 12: Jack Kornfield, "Fear and Anger," *Jack Kornfield* (blog), accessed 02/06/18, https://jackkornfield.com/fear-and-anger/.

PAGE 13: Amanda Petrusich, "Headphones Everywhere," Cultural Comment, *New Yorker*, July 12, 2016, https://www.newyorker.com/culture/cultural-comment/headphones-everywhere.

PAGE 14: Ursula K. Le Guin, *Words Are My Matter: Writings about Life and Books, 2000–2016* (Easthampton, MA: Small Beer Press, 2016), 48.

CHAPTER ONE

PAGE 16: Evan Osnos, "When Tyranny Takes Hold," *New Yorker*, December 19, 2016, https://www.newyorker.com/magazine/2016/12/19/when-tyranny-takes-hold.

PAGE 16: Joseph Folkman, "Feeling Overwhelmed? You Are Far from Alone," *Forbes*, July 23, 2015, https://www.forbes.com/sites/joefolkman/2015/07/23/feeling-overwhelmed-you-are-far-from-alone.

PAGE 16: "'Depression: Let's Talk,' Says WHO, as Depression Tops List of Causes of Ill Health," Media Centre, World Health Organization, March 30, 2017, http://www.who.int/mediacentre/news/releases/2017/world-health-day/en/.

PAGE 17: Benoit Denizet-Lewis, "Why Are More American Teenagers Than Ever Suffering from Severe Anxiety," *New York Times Magazine*, October 11, 2017.

PAGE 19: Alyssa Mastromonaco, interview by Jon Favreau et al., "This Snowflake Is Enraged," *Pod Save America*, podcast, August 31, 2017, https://art19.com/shows/pod-save-america/episodes/ddda9e4e-dbe3-400b-afb8-b125477ed92b.

PAGE 19: Dr. Bessel van der Kolk, *The Body Keeps the Score: Brain, Mind, and Body in the Healing of Trauma* (New York: Viking, 2014), 86.

PAGE 21: "Parenting," The Gottman Institute, accessed 02/06/18, https://www.gottman.com/about/research/parenting/.

PAGE 23: Katrina Yu, "Red Alert: Life Inside the Beijing Smog," Al Jazeera, January 5, 2016, http://www.aljazeera.com/indepth/features/2016/01/red-alert-life-beijing-smog-160104063026957.html.

PAGE 23: "Flint Water Crisis Fast Facts," CNN, November 28, 2017, http://www.cnn.com/2016/03/04/us/flint-water-crisis-fast-facts/index.html.

PAGE 23: Richard Louv, "No More 'Nature-Deficit Disorder': The 'No Child Left Inside' Movement," *Psychology Today*, January 28, 2009, https://www.psychologytoday.com/blog/people-in-nature/200901/no-more-nature-deficit-disorder.

PAGE 23: R. J. Mitchell et al., "Neighborhood Environments and Socioeconomic Inequalities in Mental Well-Being," *American Journal of Preventive Medicine* 49, no. 1 (July 2015): 80–84.

PAGE 24: Yuri Gama, "The Rise and Fall of an African American Inner City," Modern Cities, March 31, 2017, https://www.moderncities.com/article/2017-mar-the-rise-and-fall-of-an-african-american-inner-city/page/.

PAGE 24: Julia Craven, "Even Breathing Is a Risk in One of Orlando's Poorest Neighborhoods," *HuffPost*, January 23, 2018, https://www.huffingtonpost.com/entry/florida-poor-black-neighborhood-air-pollution_us_5a663a67e4b0e5630072746e.

PAGE 24: John Yarmuth, interview by DeRay Mckesson, "Navigating Identity and Navigating Justice," *Pod Save the People*, podcast, September 12, 2017, https://art19.com/shows/pod-save-the-people/episodes/a8393922-a802-4edb-9812-3369147b0bc5.

CHAPTER TWO

PAGE 28: Mark Epstein, "The Trauma of Being Alive," *New York Times*, August 3, 2013, http://www.nytimes.com/2013/08/04/opinion/sunday/the-trauma-of-being-alive.html.

PAGE 28: Angela Saini, "Epigenetics: Genes, Environment, and the Generation Game," *Guardian*, September 6, 2014, https://www.theguardian.com/science/2014/sep/07/epigenetics-heredity-diabetes-obesity-increased-cancer-risk.

PAGE 29: Donna Jackson Nakazawa, "Childhood, Disrupted," Aeon, July 7, 2015, https://aeon.co/essays/how-bad-experiences-in-childhood-lead-to-adult-illness.

PAGE 29: Seth D. Pollak, "Mechanisms Linking Early Experience and the Emergence of Emotions: Illustrations from the Study of Maltreated Children," *Current Directions in Psychological Science* 17, no. 6 (December 2008): 370–75.

PAGE 29: "Can Trauma Be Passed to Next Generation through DNA?" NewsHour, PBS, video, August 31, 2015, http://www.pbs.org/newshour/extra/daily-videos/can-trauma-be-passed-to-next-generation-through-dna/.

PAGE 29: Tori Rodriguez, "Descendants of Holocaust Survivors Have Altered Stress Hormones," *Scientific American*, March 1, 2015, https://www.scientificamerican.com/article/descendants-of-holocaust-survivors-have-altered-stress-hormones/.

PAGE 29: Will Storr, "A Better Kind of Happiness," *New Yorker*, July 7, 2016, https://www.newyorker.com/tech/elements/a-better-kind-of-happiness.

PAGE 30: Maureen Trudelle Schwarz, *Molded in the Image of Changing Woman: Navajo Views on the Human Body and Personhood* (Tucson: University of Arizona Press, 1997), cited in Shea Robison, "Epigenetics before Epigenetics Was Cool?" *Nexus of Epigenetics* (blog), July 30, 2014, https://nexusof epigenetics.com/2014/07/30/epigenetics-before-epigentics-was-cool/.

PAGE 31: Saul Elbein, "The Youth Group That Launched a Movement at Standing Rock," *New York Times Magazine*, January 31, 2017.

PAGE 31: Annamarya Scaccia, "The Mental and Physical Trauma of 750,000 DACA Kids Living in Limbo," *Yes Magazine*, March 3, 2017, http://www.yesmagazine.org/peace-justice/the-mental-and-physical-trauma-of-dreamers-living-with-deportation-threats-20170303.

PAGE 31: Omer Karasapan, "Syria's Mental Health Crisis," *Brookings* (blog), April 25, 2016, https://www.brookings.edu/blog/future-development/2016/04/25/syrias-mental-health-crisis/.

PAGE 33: The Sentencing Project, *Report of the Sentencing Project to the United Nations Human Rights Committee*, August 2013, http://sentencingproject.org/wp-content/uploads/2015/12/Race-and-Justice-Shadow-Report-ICCPR.pdf.

PAGE 33: "School-to-Prison Pipeline," ACLU, accessed 02/06/18, https://www.aclu.org/issues/racial-justice/race-and-inequality-education/school-prison-pipeline.

PAGE 33: Peter Wagner and Bernadette Rabuy, "Mass Incarceration: The Whole Pie 2017," Prison Policy Initiative, March 14, 2017, https://www.prisonpolicy.org/reports/pie2017.html.

PAGE 33: Alison Walsh, "The Criminal Justice System Is Riddled with Racial Disparities," *Prison Policy Initiative* (blog), August 15, 2016, https://www.prisonpolicy.org/blog/2016/08/15/cjrace/.

PAGE 33: Joshua Rovner, "Disproportionate Minority Contact in the Juvenile Justice System," Sentencing Project, May 1, 2014, http://www.sentencingproject.org/publications/disproportionate-minority-contact-in-the-juvenile-justice-system/.

PAGE 33: Carla Amurao, "Fact Sheet: How Bad Is the School-to-Prison Pipeline?" Tavis Smiley Reports, PBS, accessed 02/06/18, http://www.pbs.org/wnet/tavissmiley/tsr/education-under-arrest/school-to-prison-pipeline-fact-sheet/ (page deleted).

PAGE 33: Penal Reform International, *Global Prison Trends 2016*, May 2016, https://cdn.penalreform.org/wp-content/uploads/2016/05/Global_prison_trends_report_2016.pdf, 16.

PAGE 34: Dawn-Lyen Gardner, interview by DeRay Mckesson, "Navigating Identity and Navigating Justice," *Pod Save the People*, podcast, September 12, 2017, https://art19.com/shows/pod-save-the-people/episodes/a8393922-a802-4edb-9812-3369147b0bc5.

PAGE 35: "2015 Sleep in America™ Poll Finds Pain a Significant Challenge When It Comes to Americans' Sleep," National Sleep Foundation, March 2, 2015, https://sleepfoundation.org/media-center/press-release/2015-sleep-america-poll.

PAGE 36: Matthew Walker, interview by Terry Gross, "Sleep Scientist Warns Against Walking through Life 'in An Underslept State,'" *Fresh Air*, NPR, October 16, 2017, https://www.npr.org/templates/transcript/transcript.php?storyId=558058812.

PAGE 36: Wayne Caswell, "Sleep Statistics from *Sleepless in America*," *Modern Health Talk* (blog), April 18, 2015, http://www.mhealthtalk.com/sleepless-in-america/.

PAGE 36: "Why Do We Need Sleep?" National Sleep Foundation, accessed 02/06/18, https://sleepfoundation.org/excessivesleepiness/content/why-do-we-need-sleep.

PAGE 36: Matthew Carter, personal communication with author, September 6, 2017.

PAGE 37: Eric Fanning, interview by Tommy Vietor, "North Korea Update Then the Army's CEO," *Pod Save the World*, podcast, September 1, 2017, https://art19.com/shows/pod-save-the-world/episodes/e7f7eb7d-6f24-4764-817c-f0dc8b21aa9f.

PAGE 37: Brian Krans, "Balanced Diet," Healthline, February 12, 2016, https://www.healthline.com/health/balanced-diet#Overview1.

PAGE 37: Tom Hanks, interview by Terry Gross, "Tom Hanks Says Self-Doubt Is 'a High-Wire Act That We All Walk,'" *Fresh Air*, NPR, April 26, 2016, https://www.npr.org/templates/transcript/transcript.php?storyId=475573489.

PAGE 37: Lenny Bernstein, "Why Do We Still Eat This Way?" *Washington Post*, August 4, 2014, https://www.washingtonpost.com/news/to-your-health/wp/2014/08/04/why-do-we-still-eat-this-way/.

PAGE 37: "Eating Processed Foods," NHS [UK], January 6, 2017, https://www.nhs.uk/Livewell/Goodfood/Pages/what-are-processed-foods.aspx.

PAGE 37: Derek Bryan, "Reasons People Eat Junk Food Instead of Healthy Food," LIVESTRONG, October 3, 2017, https://www.livestrong.com/article/392358-reasons-why-people-eat-junk-food-over-healthy-food/.

PAGE 38: "Food Deserts," Centers for Disease Control and Prevention, accessed 02/06/18, https://www.cdc.gov/features/FoodDeserts/index.html.

PAGE 38: J. Gabriel Ware, "Black Neighbors Band Together to Bring in Healthy Food, Co-op-Style," *Yes Magazine*, September 11, 2017, http://www .yesmagazine.org/people-power/black-neighbors-band-together-to-bring-in-healthy-food-co-op-style-20170911.

PAGE 38: "What Is Food Justice," Just Food, accessed 02/06/18, http://justfood .org/advocacy/what-is-food-justice.

PAGE 39: Mike Lindblom, "Washington Distracted-Driving Law Has Driver Wondering if They Can Still Drink Coffee on the Road," *Seattle Times*, July 27, 2017, https://www.seattletimes.com/seattle-news/transportation/ washington-distracted-driving-law-has-drivers-wondering-if-they-can-still-drink-coffee-on-the-road/.

PAGE 40: Jean Twenge, "Have Smartphones Destroyed a Generation?" *Atlantic*, September 2017.

PAGE 40: Julianne Holt-Lunstad, "Why Loneliness Is a Public Health Threat," *Fortune*, August 7, 2017, http://fortune.com/2017/08/07/loneliness-public-health/.

PAGE 41: Jack Kornfield, personal communication with author.

PAGE 45: Sheila Nevins, interview by Alec Baldwin, "HBO's Sheila Nevins Makes Docs Hot," *Here's the Thing*, podcast, September 5, 2017, https:// www.wnycstudios.org/story/hbos-sheila-nevins-makes-docs-hot/.

PAGE 46: "Vacation Leave," U.S. Department of Labor, accessed 02/06/18, https://www.dol.gov/general/topic/workhours/vacation_leave.

PAGE 46: Lydia Dishman, "How U.S. Employee Benefits Compare to Europe's," *Fast Company*, February 17, 2016, https://www.fastcompany.com/ 3056830/how-the-us-employee-benefits-compare-to-europe.

PAGE 46: Quentin Fottrell, "The Sad Reason Half of Americans Don't Take All Their Paid Vacation," *MarketWatch*, May 28, 2017, https://www .marketwatch.com/story/55-of-american-workers-dont-take-all-their-paid-vacation-2016-06-15.

PAGE 46: Project: Time Off, *The State of American Vacation: How Vacation Became a Casualty of Our Work Culture*, 2016, https://www.projecttimeoff .com/sites/default/files/PTO_SoAV%20Report_FINAL.pdf.

PAGE 46: Colleen Story, "Cerebral Congestion—How It Ruins Your Work in Progress," *Writing and Wellness* (blog), March 18, 2014, http://www .writingandwellness.com/2014/03/18/cerebral-congestion-how-it-ruins-your-work-in-progress/.

PAGE 46: "New Survey Reveals Extent, Impact of Information Overload on Workers; From Boston to Beijing, Professionals Feel Overwhelmed, Demoralized," LexisNexis, October 20, 2010, https://www.lexisnexis.com/ en-us/about-us/media/press-release.page?id=128751276114739.

PAGE 47: Dr. William I. Robinson, "The 'Great Recession of 2008' and the Continuing Crisis: A Global Capitalism Perspective," *International Review of Modern Sociology* 38, no. 2 (Autumn 2012): 169–98.

PAGE 48: John Yarmuth, interview by DeRay Mckesson, "Navigating Identity and Navigating Justice," *Pod Save the People*, podcast, September 12, 2017, https://art19.com/shows/pod-save-the-people/episodes/a8393922-a802-4edb-9812-3369147b0bc5.

PAGE 49: "The Science Is Settled," Climate Reality Project, accessed 02/06/18, https://www.climaterealityproject.org/climate-101.

PAGE 49: Steve Inskeep, "Despite Climate Change Setbacks, Al Gore 'Comes Down on the Side of Hope,'" *Morning Edition*, NPR, July 24, 2017, https://www.npr.org/2017/07/24/538391386/despite-climate-change-setbacks-al-gore-comes-down-on-the-side-of-hope.

PAGE 49: Chris D'Angelo, "Climate Change Has 'Loaded the Dice' on the Frequency of 100-Year Floods," *HuffPost*, August 30, 2017, https://www.huffingtonpost.com/entry/100-year-flood-climate-change_us_59a6eaa3e4b084581a14ea14.

PAGE 50: Julie Beck, "Constant Anxiety Won't Save the World," *Atlantic*, August 17, 2017, https://www.theatlantic.com/health/archive/2017/08/constant-anxiety-wont-save-the-world/537132/.

PAGE 50: Josh Fox, interview by Alec Baldwin, "Josh Fox," *Here's the Thing*, podcast, July 8, 2013, https://www.wnycstudios.org/story/299366-josh-fox/.

CHAPTER THREE

PAGE 55: Adam Gopnik, "Talking to Kids about Trump's Victory," *New Yorker*, November 9, 2017, https://www.newyorker.com/news/news-desk/talking-to-kids-about-trumps-victory.

PAGE 55: Stevie Wonder, live performance, White River Amphitheatre, Auburn, Washington. July 11, 2008.

PAGE 55: Quoted by Gary Snyder, interview with Peter Barry Chowka, *East West Journal*, June 1977.

PAGE 58: Jack Kornfield, personal communication with author.

PAGE 59: Parker J. Palmer, *A Hidden Wholeness: The Journey toward an Undivided Life* (San Francisco: Jossey-Bass, 2009), 5.

PAGE 60: Jean-Paul Sartre, *Saint Genet: Actor and Martyr*, trans. Bernard Frechtman (Minneapolis: University of Minnesota Press, 2012), 584.

PAGE 63: James Clear, "This Coach Improved Every Tiny Thing by 1 Percent and Here's What Happened," *James Clear* (blog), accessed 02/06/18, https://jamesclear.com/marginal-gains.

PAGE 63: Timothy Ferriss, *Tools of Titans: The Tactics, Routines, and Habits of Billionaires, Icons, and World-Class Performers* (New York: Houghton Mifflin, 2016), 627.

CHAPTER FOUR

PAGE 66: Aldous Huxley, *Brave New World Revisited* (New York: Harper, 1958).

PAGE 67: Paul Lewis, "'Our Minds Can Be Hijacked': The Tech Insiders Who Fear a Smartphone Dystopia," *Guardian*, October 6, 2017, https://www.theguardian.com/technology/2017/oct/05/smartphone-addiction-silicon-valley-dystopia.

PAGE 67: "The Mere Presence of Your Smartphone Reduces Brain Power, Study Shows," *UT News*, June 26, 2017, https://news.utexas.edu/2017/06/26/the-mere-presence-of-your-smartphone-reduces-brain-power.

PAGE 68: Rebecca Coxon, "Overwhelming Technology Disrupting Life and Causing Stress New Study Shows," Mental Healthy, accessed 02/06/18, http://www.mentalhealthy.co.uk/news/568-overwhelming-technology-disrupting-life-and-causing-stress-new-study-shows.html.

PAGE 68: Andrew Hough, "Student 'Addiction' to Technology 'Similar to Drug Cravings', Study Finds," *Telegraph*, April 8, 2011, http://www.telegraph.co.uk/technology/news/8436831/Student-addiction-to-technology-similar-to-drug-cravings-study-finds.html.

PAGE 68: Stephen Colbert, interview by Terry Gross, "'Late Show' Host Says He Has Finally Found His Post-'Colbert Report' Voice," *Fresh Air*, NPR, November 2, 2016, https://www.npr.org/templates/transcript/transcript.php?storyId=500303201.

PAGE 69: Clint Smith, interview by DeRay Mckesson, "Navigating Identity and Navigating Justice," *Pod Save the People*, podcast, September 12, 2017, https://art19.com/shows/pod-save-the-people/episodes/a8393922-a802-4edb-9812-3369147b0bc5.

PAGE 69: Benoit Denizet-Lewis, "Why Are More American Teenagers Than Ever Suffering from Severe Anxiety," *New York Times Magazine*, October 11, 2017.

PAGE 70: Glynis Ratcliffe, "The Teen Anxiety Epidemic: Social Media Is Here to Stay but at What Cost?" *ParentMap*, September 18, 2017, https://www.parentmap.com/article/teen-anxiety-epidemic.

PAGE 71: Alan Watts, *Does It Matter? Essays on Man's Relation to Materiality* (New York: Pantheon, 1970).

PAGE 72: Rick Hanson, "Feel Already Full," *Dr. Rick Hanson* (blog), accessed 02/06/18, http://www.rickhanson.net/feel-already-full/.

PAGE 73: Maria Popova, "Leonard Bernstein on Cynicism, Instant Gratification, and Why Paying Attention Is a Countercultural Act of Courage and Rebellion," *Brain Pickings* (blog), October 3, 2016, https://www.brainpickings .org/2016/10/03/dinner-with-lenny-leonard-bernstein-jonathan-cott/.

PAGE 73: James Baldwin, *Notes of a Native Son* (Boston: Beacon Press, 1955).

PAGE 74: Martha C. Nussbaum, *Anger and Forgiveness: Resentment, Generosity, Justice* (Oxford: Oxford University Press, 2016).

PAGE 74: Dr. Richard Davidson, personal communication with author and Marianne Spoon. November 8, 2017.

PAGE 75: John Feal, interview by Terry Gross, "Sept. 11 First Responder Fights on Behalf of Others Who Rushed to Help," *Fresh Air*, NPR, September 11, 2017, https://www.npr.org/templates/transcript/transcript.php?storyId= 550094607.

PAGE 76: Jon Lovett, "Trump's Emotional Affair," *Lovett or Leave It*, podcast, September 16, 2017, https://art19.com/shows/lovett-or-leave-it/episodes/ 039f8a30-41b5-49ae-9f7a-c9523d8b4cb0.

PAGE 77: NPR/Robert Wood Johnson Foundation/Harvard School of Public Health, *The Burden of Stress in America*, 2014, accessed 02/06/18, https:// www.rwjf.org/content/dam/farm/reports/surveys_and_polls/2014/ rwjf414295.

PAGE 77: John O'Donohue, *Beauty: The Invisible Embrace* (New York: HarperCollins, 2004).

PAGE 78: Willa Paskin, "Secret Agent Mandy," *New York*, September 9, 2012, http://nymag.com/arts/tv/fall-2012/mandy-patinkin-2012-9/.

PAGE 79: Julie Beck, "Constant Anxiety Won't Save the World," *Atlantic*, August 17, 2017, https://www.theatlantic.com/health/archive/2017/08/constant-anxiety-wont-save-the-world/537132/.

PAGE 80: Mohsin Hamid, interview by Terry Gross, "From Refugees to Politics, Mohsin Hamid Writes the Change He Wants to See," *Fresh Air*, NPR, March 8, 2017, https://www.npr.org/templates/transcript/transcript .php?storyId=519217991.

PAGES 81–82: Paul Lewis, "'Our Minds Can Be Hijacked': The Tech Insiders Who Fear a Smartphone Dystopia," *Guardian*, October 6, 2017, https:// www.theguardian.com/technology/2017/oct/05/smartphone-addiction-silicon-valley-dystopia.

PAGE 83: Karen Young, "The Science of Gratitude—How It Changes People, Relationships (and Brains!) and How to Make It Work for You," *Hey Sigmund* (blog), accessed 02/06/18, https://www.heysigmund.com/ the-science-of-gratitude/.

PAGE 83: Jesse Walker, Amit Kumar, and Thomas Gilovich, "Cultivating Gratitude and Giving through Experiential Consumption," *Emotion* 16, no. 8 (December 2016): 1126–36.

PAGE 83: Emily Gersema, "Researchers Design a Study to Track Gratitude," *USC News*, October 19, 2015, https://news.usc.edu/87605/researchers-design-a-brain-scan-study-to-track-gratitude/.

PAGE 84: Colin Warner, interview by DeRay Mckesson, "On Their Shoulders," *Pod Save the People*, podcast, August 22, 2017, https://art19.com/shows/pod-save-the-people/episodes/3e2dc899-ab55-4e26-8bd9-5982c1c20256.

PAGE 84: Dalai Lama, Desmond Tutu, and Douglas Abrams, *The Book of Joy: Lasting Happiness in a Changing World* (New York: Avery, 2016).

PAGE 85: Maria Popova, "John Steinbeck on Good and Evil, the Necessary Contradictions of the Human Nature, and Our Grounds for Lucid Hope," *Brain Pickings* (blog), December 30, 2016, https://www.brainpickings.org/2016/12/30/john-steinbeck-new-year/.

PAGE 87: Richard Elman, review of *A Rap on Race*, by Margaret Mead and James Baldwin, *New York Times*, June 27, 1971.

CHAPTER FIVE

PAGE 92: Sheryll Cashin, interview by Terry Gross, "50 Years Later, 'Loving' Revisits the Landmark Supreme Court Ruling," *Fresh Air*, NPR, June 5, 2017, https://www.npr.org/2017/06/05/531578449/50-years-later-loving-revisits-the-landmark-supreme-court-ruling.

PAGE 96: Giancarlo Esposito, interview by Terry Gross, "'Better Call Saul' Actor Giancarlo Esposito on the Making of an Iconic Villain," *Fresh Air*, NPR, June 7, 2017, https://www.npr.org/templates/transcript/transcript.php?storyId=531840764.

PAGE 97: Maria Popova, "The Science of How Our Minds and Our Bodies Converge in the Healing of Trauma," *Brain Pickings* (blog), June 20, 2016, https://www.brainpickings.org/2016/06/20/the-body-keeps-the-score-van-der-kolk/.

PAGE 97: Linda Sparrowe, "Transcending Trauma: How Yoga Heals," Yoga International, accessed 02/06/18, https://yogainternational.com/article/view/transcending-trauma-how-yoga-heals.

PAGE 97: B. Rael Cahn et al., "Yoga, Meditation and Mind-Body Health: Increased BDNF, Cortisol Awakening Response, and Altered Inflammatory Marker Expression after a 3-Month Yoga and Meditation Retreat," *Frontiers in Human Neuroscience*, 11 (June 26, 2017): 315.

PAGE 98: Bruce Springsteen, *Born to Run* (New York: Simon and Schuster, 2016).

PAGE 98: Kirsten Weir, "The Exercise Effect," *Monitor on Psychology* 42, no. 11 (December 2011): 48.

PAGE 98: "Benefits of Exercise," NHS [UK], accessed 02/06/18, https://www.nhs.uk/Livewell/fitness/Pages/Whybeactive.aspx.

PAGE 98: "What Is Exercise Is Medicine," Exercise Is Medicine, http://www.exerciseismedicine.org/support_page.php/about/.

PAGE 99: Jennifer Welsh, "Scientists Have Finally Found the First Real Reason We Need to Sleep," Business Insider, October 17, 2013, http://www.businessinsider.com/the-first-real-reason-we-need-to-sleep-2013-10.

PAGE 99: Lulu Xie et al., "Sleep Drives Metabolite Clearance from the Adult Brain," *Science*, October 18, 2013, 373–77.

PAGE 100: Juyoung Lee et al., "Influence of Forest Therapy on Cardiovascular Relaxation in Young Adults," *Evidence-Based Complementary and Alternative Medicine* 2014 (2014). http://doi.org/10.1155/2014/834360.

PAGE 100: Rahawa Haile, "'Forest Bathing': How Microdosing on Nature Can Help with Stress," *Atlantic*, June 30, 2017, https://www.theatlantic.com/health/archive/2017/06/forest-bathing/532068/.

PAGE 101: Maya Shetreat-Klein, "The Dirt Cure," PCC Community Markets, September 2017, https://www.pccmarkets.com/sound-consumer/2017-09/the-dirt-cure/.

PAGE 101: Tik Root, "Doctors Are Prescribing Park Visits to Boost Patient Health," *National Geographic*, June 29, 2017, https://news.nationalgeographic.com/2017/06/parks-prescribes-doctors-health-environment/.

PAGE 101: James Hamblin, "The Nature Cure," *Atlantic*, October 2015.

PAGE 101: Seth and Jane Chang, "Research Compiled by NEEF," January 2016, https://docs.google.com/document/d/1L1SsvK3cgrr-Fk0QBdBpzSM4cJXiJManiGhDtV-__EA/edit.

PAGE 102: Sy Montgomery, "Psychological Effects of Pets Are Profound," *Boston Globe*, January 12, 2015, https://www.bostonglobe.com/lifestyle/2015/01/12/your-brain-pets/geoJHAfFHxrwNS4OgWb7sO/story.html.

CHAPTER SIX

PAGE 105: Thich Nhat Hanh, dharma talk.

PAGE 109: Bryan Stevenson, Seattle Arts & Lectures, Benaroya Hall, Seattle, Washington. March 28, 2017.

PAGE 110: Benoit Denizet-Lewis, "Why Are More American Teenagers Than Ever Suffering from Severe Anxiety," *New York Times Magazine*, October 11, 2017.

PAGE 110: John O'Donohue, *Conamara Blues* (New York: Harper Perennial, 2004).

PAGE 111: Ken Burns, interview by Marc Maron, "Ken Burns and Lynn Novick," *WTF with Marc Maron*, podcast, September 11, 2017, http://www.wtfpod.com/podcast/episode-845-ken-burns-lynn-novick.

PAGE 112: Doug Lute, interview by Tommy Vietor, "War Policy," *Pod Save the World*, podcast, September 6, 2017, https://art19.com/shows/pod-save-the-world/episodes/50262131-5c49-4c41-9852-ee699bc7ef71.

PAGE 112: Thomas L. Friedman, "How to Get a Job at Google," *New York Times*, February 22, 2014.

PAGE 113-114: Private family files.

PAGE 114: Cory Booker, "Commencement Address," University of Pennsylvania, May 15, 2017, transcript available at http://time.com/4779661/senator-cory-booker-new-jersey-university-of-pennsylvania-upenn/.

PAGE 115: Rebecca Solnit, *Hope in the Dark: Untold Histories, Wild Possibilities* (New York: Nation Books, 2004).

PAGE 116: Scott Horton, "Merton—the Value of Essential Works," *Browsings* (blog), *Harper's Magazine*, January 23, 2010, https://harpers.org/blog/2010/01/merton-the-value-of-essential-works/.

PAGE 116: Kevin Jon Heller, "How to Prosecute a War Criminal," *New Yorker Radio Hour*, WNYC, April 15, 2016, https://www.wnyc.org/story/how-prosecute-war-criminal-rerun/.

PAGE 116: Anne Barnard, Ben Hubbard, and Ian Fisher, "As Atrocities Mount in Syria, Justice Seems Out of Reach," *New York Times*, April 15, 2017, https://www.nytimes.com/2017/04/15/world/middleeast/syria-bashar-al-assad-evidence.html.

PAGE 117: Maria Popova, "Rosanne Cash on How Science Saved Her Life, the Source of Every Artist's Power, and Her Beautiful Reading of Adrienne Rich's Tribute to Marie Curie," *Brain Pickings* (blog), May 2, 2017, https://www.brainpickings.org/2017/05/02/rosanne-cash-adrienne-rich-marie-curie/.

PAGE 117: Elizabeth Kolbert, "Why Facts Don't Change Our Minds," *New Yorker*, February 27, 2017.

PAGE 117: Steven Sloman and Philip Fernbach, *The Knowledge Illusion: Why We Never Think Alone* (New York: Riverhead Books, 2017).

PAGE 117: Walt Whitman, "Song of Myself," *Leaves of Grass: The Original 1855 Edition* (Nashville, TN: American Renaissance Books, 2009), 63.

PAGE 118: Sara Gorman and Jack Gorman, *Denying to the Grave: Why We Ignore the Facts That Will Save Us* (New York: Oxford University Press, 2017).

PAGE 118: Bill Moyers, interview by Terry Gross, "Bill Moyers on Working with LBJ to Pass Medicare 52 Years Ago," *Fresh Air*, NPR, August 3, 2017, https://www.npr.org/2017/08/03/541278161/bill-moyers-on-working-with-lbj-to-pass-medicare-52-years-ago.

PAGE 118: "Read Laurie Anderson's Moving Rock Hall Speech for Lou Reed," *Rolling Stone*, April 19, 2015, https://www.rollingstone.com/music/news/read-laurie-andersons-moving-rock-hall-speech-for-lou-reed-20150419.

PAGE 118: Carl Sagan, *The Demon-Haunted World: Science as a Candle in the Dark* (New York: Ballantine, 1996).

CHAPTER SEVEN

PAGE 121: Matthew Walker, interview by Terry Gross, "Sleep Scientist Warns Against Walking through Life 'in an Underslept State,'" *Fresh Air*, NPR, October 16, 2017, https://www.npr.org/ templates/transcript/transcript .php?storyId=558058812.

PAGE 121: "Why Do We Sleep Anyway?" Healthy Sleep, http://healthysleep .med.harvard.edu/healthy/matters/benefits-of-sleep/why-do-we-sleep.

PAGE 123: John Tierney, "Do You Suffer from Decision Fatigue?" *New York Times Magazine*, August 17, 2011.

PAGE 125: Larry Chang, comp. and ed. *Wisdom for the Soul: Five Millennia of Prescriptions for Spiritual Healing* (Washington, DC: Gnosophia, 2006), 234.

PAGE 126: Peter Berg, interview by Dave Davies, "'Deepwater Horizon' Director on the BP Oil Spill and the 'Addictive Dance' for Fuel," *Fresh Air*, NPR, September 26, 2016, https://www.npr.org/2016/09/26/495467460/deepwater-horizon-director-on-the-bp-oil-spill-and-the-addictive-dance-for-fuel.

PAGE 126: Cleve Jones, interview by Terry Gross, "LGBTQ Activist Cleve Jones: 'I'm Well Aware How Fragile Life Is'," *Fresh Air*, NPR, November 29, 2016, https://www.npr.org/templates/transcript/transcript.php?storyId=503724044.

PAGE 127: Thich Nhat Hanh, *Call Me by My True Names: The Collected Poems of Thich Nhat Hanh* (Berkeley, CA: Parallax Press, 1999).

PAGE 127: Matt Fitzgerald, *How Bad Do You Want It?* (Boulder, CO: VeloPress, 2015).

PAGE 128: Nick Heil, "Why Mindfulness Is Your New Secret Weapon," *Outside*, March 22, 2016, https://www.outsideonline.com/2063611/why-mindfulness-your-new-secret-weapon.

PAGE 128: Sarah Wightman, "What Limits Endurance Performance? The Science of Fatigue," *Flying Runner* (blog), April 21, 2017, https://www.flyingrunner .co.uk/science-of-fatigue/.

PAGE 128: Sam Murphy, "Science of Suffering," *Runners World*, August 12, 2016, https://www.runnersworld.co.uk/training/science-of-suffering.

PAGE 129: Ralph Waldo Emerson, "Merlin's Song," *Poems* (Boston: Houghton

Mifflin, 1904), 219.

PAGE 130: Bruce Springsteen, *Born to Run* (New York: Simon and Schuster, 2016), 359.

PAGE 131: Gus Lubin, "Psychologists: Awesomeness Is Good for You," Business Insider, June 5, 2012, http://www.businessinsider.com/psychologists-awesomeness-is-good-for-you-2012-6.

PAGE 131: Bryan Stevenson, Seattle Arts & Lectures, Benaroya Hall, Seattle, Washington. March 28, 2017.

PAGE 133: William Faulkner, speech at the Nobel Banquet, December 10, 1950, Stockholm, transcript available at https://www.nobelprize.org/nobel_prizes/literature/laureates/1949/faulkner-speech.html.

PAGE 134: Aldous Huxley, *Music at Night and Other Essays* (New York: Fountain Press, 1931).

PAGE 135: Michael Paulson, "'Hamilton' and Heartache: Living the Unimaginable," *New York Times*, October 13, 2016.

PAGE 138: Nick Paumgarten, "Life Is Rescues: Looking for Trouble with a National Team of Emergency-Response Volunteers," *New Yorker*, November 9, 2015.

PAGE 139: Yanan Wang, "A Compassionate Judge Sentences a Veteran to 24 Hours in Jail, Then Joins Him behind Bars," *Washington Post*, April 22, 2016, https://www.washingtonpost.com/news/morning-mix/wp/2016/04/22/a-judge-sentences-a-veteran-to-24-hours-in-jail-then-joins-him-behind-bars/.

PAGE 139: Martin Buber, *Pointing the Way: Collected Essays* (Humanity Books: New York, 1999), 28, quoted in Israel Koren, *The Mystery of the Earth: Mysticism and Hasidism in the Thought of Martin Buber* (Brill: Leiden, The Netherlands, 2010), 148.

PAGE 139: Robert Brault, "Who Wrote Enjoy the Little Things....?," *New Robert Brault Reader* (blog), accessed 02/06/18, http://rbrault.blogspot.com/p/who-wrote-enjoy-little-things.html.

CHAPTER EIGHT

PAGE 143: Jack Kornfield, "The Zen of an Aching Heart," *Jack Kornfield* (blog), accessed 02/06/18, https://jackkornfield.com/zen-aching-heart/.

PAGE 145: Tim Krieder, "The 'Busy' Trap," *Opinionator* (blog), *New York Times*, June 30, 2012, https://opinionator.blogs.nytimes.com/2012/06/30/the-busy-trap/.

PAGE 146: Joe Berlinger, interview by Alec Baldwin, "Joe Berlinger," *Here's the Thing*, podcast, January 16, 2012, https://www.wnycstudios.org/story/

176623-joe-berlinger/.

PAGE 146: Jack Kornfield, *The Wise Heart: A Guide to the Universal Teachings of Buddhist Psychology* (New York: Bantam, 2008).

PAGE 147: "Dinos Christianopoulos Quotes," Goodreads, https://www .goodreads.com/quotes/7370898-they-tried-to-bury-us-they-didn-t-know-we-were.

PAGE 149: Connie Burk, personal communication with author, 2017, Seattle, Washington.

PAGE 151: Thich Nhat Hanh, dharma talk.

CONCLUSION

PAGE 154: "Oprah Talks to Elie Wiesel," *O, The Oprah Magazine*, November 2000, http://www.oprah.com/omagazine/oprah-interviews-elie-wiesel/all.

INDEX

A

Abrams, Douglas, 84

Abuse and assault victims, 59, 132

Activism. *See* Political organizing and
    activism

Addiction
    detoxing in, 95–96
    to screen time and social media, 67, 68,
        81, 96

Adenosine, 121

Aggregation of marginal gains, 63

Albarracin, Dolores, 79

Anabolism, 54

Anderson, Laurie, 118

Anger
    cynicism in, 72–74
    media appealing to, 82

Animals, benefits of spending time with,
    101–102

Anxiety, 78–79, 80, 98

Apartheid, 10–11, 55, 60

Art, to improve stamina, 133–135

Ashworth, Kevin, 110

Attachment, 62, 103–118

Attention
    continuous partial, in distraction, 67
    economy of, 82
    and presence, 94–95

Augustine of Hippo, Saint, 7

B

Backpacking, 154

Baldwin, James, 11, 73, 87

Baumeister, Roy, 123

Beck, Julie, 78

Beginner's mind, 109, 117

Berg, Peter, 125–126

Berlinger, Joe, 145–146

Bernstein, Leonard, 72–73

Bias
    confirmation, 118
    negativity, 71, 80

Bock, Laszlo, 112

Booker, Cory, 114

Brain
    caffeine affecting, 121
    circuits to influence well-being, 74
    in decision fatigue and ego depletion,
        122–123
    in effort perception, 127–128
    emotion and logical centers in, 7
    in fight-or-flight reaction, 125
    in negativity bias, 71

Brault, Robert, 139

Breathing in meditation, 96

Brichter, Loren, 81

Brown, Grace, 131

Brulé, Robin, 150

Buber, Martin, 139

Buddhism, 11, 109

Burk, Connie, xiii–xiv, 5, 149

Burns, Ken, 111

C

Caffeine, 95, 120–122

Cape Town, South Africa, District Six in,
    10–11

Carter, Matthew, 36

Cash, Rosanne, 117

Cashin, Sheryll, 91–92

Catabolism, 54
Causes of overwhelm, 27–51
    barriers in response to, 57–60
    less as more in response to, 60–63
    metabolizing exposure to, 53, 54–55,
        62
    saturation of, 55–56, 62
Chah, Ajahn, 12
Charger, Jasilyn, 31
Chödrön, Pema, 61
Choice
    decision fatigue in, 122–124
    in intentional behavior, 8–14, 60–62,
        66, 74–87
    to step away, 143–151
Christianopoulos, Dinos, 147
Climate crisis, 49–51, 115
Clutter, simplifying in, 125
Colbert, Stephen, 68
Cole, Steve, 29–30
Collective control, 4–5, 11, 114
Community and neighborhood, 22–25
    engagement with, 137–141
    food available in, 38
    housing and zoning policies in, 23–24
    immigrants and refugees in, 24–25
    staying in or stepping away from, 148–
        149
    violence in, 25
Compassion, 11, 28
Confirmation bias, 118
Connection, 62, 89–102
    with animals, 101–102
    with community, 137–141
    detoxing practice for, 95–96
    eudaimonic happiness in, 29
    meditation and yoga for, 96–97
    with nature, 100–101
    physical activity for, 97–99
    screen time and social media affecting,
        39–40, 66–67, 70
    sleep for, 99–100
Craven, Julia, 24
Creating conditions, 11–14
Curiosity, 62, 105, 109–118
    in beginner's mind, 109, 117
    humility in, 111–113
    openness in, 109–110
    and self-respect, 116–118

Cynicism, 72–74
Czeisler, Charles, 99

D
Daily routines
    detoxing in, 95–96
    gratitude in, 84
    intention in, 76–78
    simplifying of, 124–125
Dakota Access Pipeline protest, 30–31
Damasio, Antonio, 83
Davidson, Richard, 74
Death
    disconnection in, 91, 93
    in family, 42–43, 76, 140–141, 150–
        151
    suicide, 17, 31, 43, 93
Decision making
    fatigue and depletion in, 122–124
    in intentional behavior, 8–14, 60–62,
        66, 74–87
    in stepping away, 143–151
Democracy, 5
Denizet-Lewis, Benoit, 17, 69
Depletion, 62, 119–141
    art appreciation in, 133–135
    building stamina in, 62, 120, 124–141
    caffeine use in, 120–122
    community engagement in, 137–141
    decision fatigue in, 122–124
    ego depletion, 123
    humor in, 136
    mind and body connection in, 125–129
    muscle fatigue in, 127
    outdoor and nature time in, 129–131
    perceived effort in, 127–128
    simplifying in, 124–125
    spirituality and religion in, 131–133
Depression, 16
Detoxing, daily practice of, 95–96
Detroit MI, food deserts in, 38
Diabetes, 37
Didion, Joan, 8
Diet, 37–39, 95–96
Discipline
    to maintain perspective, 85–87
    and limits to self-control, 123
Disconnection, 62, 89–102. *See also*
    Connection

Discrimination, in housing and zoning policies, 23–24
Distraction, 62, 65–87
    in anticipation of trouble, 71
    continuous partial attention in, 67
    cynicism in, 72–74
    decision fatigue in, 123
    as escape, 60
    intentional focus in, 60, 62, 66, 74–87
    limits to self-control in, 123
    managing volume and intensity of, 78–83
    in memory of past and fantasy of future, 71
    sleep problems in, 99
    in social media use and screen time, 66–70, 80–83
District Six of Cape Town, South Africa, 10–11
DNA and epigenetics, 28–30
Dopamine, 65, 81, 83, 102, 118
Drinking water, lead in, 23
DuVernay, Ava, 34

E
Ebrahim, Noor, 10–11
Edwards-Teasley, ShaKiana, 140
Effort, perception of, 127–128
Ego depletion, 123
Emergency responders, 74–75, 137–138
Emerson, Ralph Waldo, 129
Endurance athletes, 127–128
Entrenchment, 62, 103–118. See also Attachment
Environmental factors, 22–25, 47–51
    and benefits of time spent outside, 23, 100–101, 129–131, 154
    climate change in, 49–51, 115
    economic stressors in, 47–48
    in epigenetics, 28–29
    housing and zoning policies in, 23–24
    natural disasters in, 18–19, 50, 51
    pollution in, 22–24, 50
    world events in, 48–49
Epigenetics, 28–30
Epstein, Mark, 28
Escape, feeling need for, 60
Esposito, Giancarlo, 96
Eudaimonic happiness, 29–30
Eustis, Oskar, 134–135

Exercise. See Physical activity
Exposure to causes of overwhelm
    barriers in management of, 57–60
    metabolizing of, 53, 54–55, 62
    saturation in, 55–56, 62, 65
Eyal, Nir, 81–82

F
Facebook, 67
Family, 20–22, 40–43
    death and grief in, 42–43, 140–141, 150–151
Famine survivors, epigenetic changes in, 29
Fatigue and depletion, 62, 119–141. See also Depletion
Faulkner, William, 133
Feal, John, 74–75
Fear
    of missing out, 69
    spread of, in trending issues, 78–79
Fernbach, Philip, 117
Ferriss, Tim, 63
Fight-or-flight response, 28, 56, 125
Fitzgerald, Matt, 127
Flint MI water supply, 23
Food choices, 37–39, 95–96
Food deserts, 38
Fox, Josh, 50
Fredrickson, Barbara, 29

G
Gardner, Dawn-Lyen, 33–34
Gasland II (film), 50
Generations
    oppression and trauma legacy in, 30–31
    relationship and family overwhelm in, 21–22
Gentrification, 24
Gladwell, Malcolm, 9
Goldman, Robin, 4
Goodwin, Doris Kearns, 86
Gopnik, Adam, 55
Gorman, Jack, 117–118
Gorman, Sara, 117–118
Gossip, 69
Gratitude, 83–85
Greed, 109

Grief, 42–43, 76
  in miscarriage, 85–86
Gulf oil spill, 50

H
Hafiz (Sufi poet), 12
Hamid, Mohsin, 79–80
Hanks, Tom, 37
Hanson, Rick, 7, 71–72
Happiness, eudaimonic, 29–30
Harm
  in disconnection, 91–92
  mitigation of, 9, 10, 58
  in saturation from exposures, 56
Health, 34–40
  diet affecting, 37–39
  outdoor time affecting, 100–101
  physical activity affecting, 98–99
  screen time and social media affecting,
    39–40
  sleep affecting, 35–37, 99
Heller, Kevin Jon, 116
Hemorrhaging in saturation from
    exposures, 56
Holocaust survivors, 10, 29
Holt-Lunstad, Julianne, 40
Housing policies, racial segregation in,
    23–24
Huerta, Dolores, 9
Human rights of prisoners, 32–33
Humility, 28, 107, 111–113
Humor
  in barriers to change, 57
  cynical, 72, 136
  to improve stamina, 128, 136
  increased intentionality, 72
Hurricane Harvey, 18–19
Huxley, Aldous, 65–66, 134

I
Iceland, search and rescue personnel in,
    137–138
Identity, attachment to, 106–107
Immigrants, 24–25, 31
Impulsive behavior, 87, 123
Individual control, 4–12
  of health, 35
  stamina in focus on, 124
Information overload, 46–47

Intentional behavior, 8–14, 60–62, 66,
    74–87
  clarifying goals of, 113–116
  in community engagement, 140–141
  in daily routines, 76–78
  discipline in, 85–87
  ego depletion affecting, 123
  gratitude in, 83–85
  and impulsive behavior, 87
  in technology use, 80–83
  volume and intensity of distractions
    affecting, 78–83
Interbeing, nature of, 4
Intergenerational oppression and trauma,
    30–31
Intergenerational relationship and family
    overwhelm, 21–22
Internalized oppression, 31, 34
Interoception, 97
Isolation, 18
  community engagement preventing,
    137–141
  health effects of, 40
  in social media use, 20, 40

J
Jones, Cleve, 126
Jordan, Chris, 50
Jordan, Vernon, 9

K
Kaufman, Joan, 28
Kessler, David, 37
Kornfield, Jack, 12, 41, 58
Kreider, Tim, 145

L
Lawson, Jenny, 136
Lead in drinking water, 23
Le Guin, Ursula K., 14
Less is more, 3, 14, 60–63
  in simplifying, 124–125
Lewis, Paul, 81
Lilly, Tina and Mark, 107
Lipsky, Jonah, 97
Loneliness
  community engagement in, 139–140
  screen time and social media affecting,
    40, 70

Lorde, Audre, 4
Louv, Richard, 23
Lovett, Jon, 76
Lute, Doug, 111–112

M

Maksimow, Cara, 70
Mann, Michael, 49
Marcora, Samuele, 127
Mastromonaco, Alyssa, 18–19
Mckesson, DeRay, 24
Meditation
    to be present, 96–97
    to improve stamina, 128, 132
Memory, sleep affecting, 36
Merton, Thomas, 116
Metabolizing exposure, 53, 54–55, 62
Military
    humility in, 111–112
    sleep deprivation in, 37
Milk, Harvey, 126
Mind and body connection, 125–129
Mindfulness, 128
Miranda, Lin-Manuel, 134–135
Miscarriage, 85–86
Moeller, Susan, 68
Morrison, Toni, 3
Moyers, Bill, 118
Music, benefits, 134–135

N

Natural disasters, 18–19, 50, 51
Nature, spending time in, 23, 154
    to be present, 100–101
    to improve stamina, 129–131
Nature-deficit disorder, 23
Negativity bias, 71, 80
Neighborhood. *See* Community and
    neighborhood
Nevins, Sheila, 45
News of world events, 48–49
    and attention economy, 82
    constant monitoring of, 96
    as distraction, 68–69, 76
    misinformation and disinformation in, 118
    as stress, 77, 96
Nhat Hanh, Thich, 4, 55, 105, 127, 151
9/11 attacks, 29, 74–75
Numbness, 90

Nussbaum, Martha, 74
Nutrition, 37–39, 95–96

O

O'Donohue, John, 77, 110
Olivera, Lou, 138–139
One Mind Youth Movement, 31
Opioid crisis, 24
Oppression, 31–34
    intergenerational transmission of legacy,
        30
    internalized, 31, 34
    systematic, 3, 31–34
Orlando, FL, Parramore neighborhood of,
        23–24
Osnos, Evan, 16
Outdoor time, 154
    to be present, 100–101
    to improve stamina, 129–131
    and nature-deficit disorder, 23
Overwhelm sensation or feeling, 1–3
    attachment in, 62, 103–118
    causes of, 27–51
    in community and society, 22–25
    continuum of, 2, 16, 17, 19
    control in, 4–7
    depletion in, 62, 119–141
    disconnection in, 40, 62, 89–102
    distraction in, 62, 65–87
    environmental factors in, 18–19, 22–24,
        47–51
    epigenetics in, 28–30
    in family, 20–22, 40–43
    intentional behavior in response to,
        8–14, 74–87
    personal, 16–20
    in schools, 17, 25, 43–45
    self-awareness of, 19–20
    in social media use, 20–21, 39–40, 44
    in workplace, 17, 45–47

P

Pacing and stamina, 124
Pain, intergenerational transmission of, 30
Palmer, Parker, 59
Parramore neighborhood of Orlando, FL,
        23–24
Patinkin, Mandy, 78
Paulson, Michael, 135

Paumgarten, Nick, 137–138
Pembrey, Marcus, 28
Perceived effort, 127–128
Perfection, striving for, 59
Personal overwhelm, 16–20
Petrusich, Amanda, 13
Physical activity
    perceived effort in, 127
    and presence in disconnection, 97–99
    and stamina in depletion, 125–126,
        127–129, 130
Plato, 125
Political organizing and activism
    clarifying intentions in, 113–114
    stamina in, 126
    staying in or stepping away from, 147
Pollak, Seth, 28–29
Pollution, 22–24, 50
Popova, Maria, 73, 85
Prejudice, 31–32
Presence, 62, 90, 92–102
    animals as positive impact on, 101–102
    detoxing practice for, 95–96
    meditation and yoga practice for, 96–97
    outdoor time for, 100–101
    physical activity for, 97–99
    sleep for, 99–100
Pride, 106
Prison system, 32–33
Psychobiology, 127

R
Racial issues
    community and society overwhelm in,
        23–24
Rakoff, David, 136
Redlining practice, 23
Reed, Lou, 118
Refugees, 24–25, 31
Relationships, 20–22
    connection in. See Connection
    curiosity and self-respect in, 117
    family. See Family
    with self, 58–60
    social media affecting, 67, 70
Religion and spirituality, 131–133
Response to causes of overwhelm
    barriers in, 57–60
    less as more in, 60–63

metabolizing exposure in, 53, 54–55, 62
    relieving saturation in, 55–56, 62
Rest time
    to improve stamina, 132–133
    and need to step away, 143–151
Robinson, William, 47
Robison, Shea, 30
Rosenstein, Justin, 67
Rudd, Melanie, 131

S
Sagan, Carl, 118
Sartre, Jean-Paul, 60
Saturation of exposures, 55–56, 62, 65
Schools, 17, 43–45
    and prison pipeline, 33
    sleep deprivation of students in, 36
    stress related to, 44
    violence in, 25
Screen time
    addiction to, 67, 68, 81, 96
    as distraction, 66–70, 80–83
    health effects of, 39–40
    intentional use of, 80–82
Search and rescue units in Iceland, 137–
        138
Self-acceptance, 58–60
Self-awareness
    of attachment, 105
    of overwhelm, 17–20
Self-control
    in distractions, 85–87
    limits to, 123
Self-respect, 116–118
September 11 attacks, 29, 74–75
Serotonin, 83, 98, 101, 119
Sessō, Oda, 55
Sexual assault victim, vulnerability feeling
        of, 59
Shetreat-Klein, Maya, 100–101
Simplifying, 124–125
Sleep
    and ability to be present, 99–100
    caffeine affecting, 121
    and health, 35–37
Sloman, Steven, 117
Smartphone use
    as distraction, 66–70
    health effects of, 39–40

illusion of control and certainty in, 110
intentional, 80–82
Smith, Clint, 69
Social media, 20–21
    addiction to, 67, 68, 81
    as distraction, 66–70, 80–83
    and fear of missing out, 69
    health effects of, 39–40
    news of world events in, 48, 68–69
    and school-related stress, 44
Society and community overwhelm, 22–25
Soil contact, benefits of, 100–101
Solnit, Rebecca, 114, 115
South Africa, Apartheid in, 10–11, 55, 60
Spirituality and religion, 131–133
Springsteen, Bruce, 98, 130
Stamina, 62, 120, 124–141
    art appreciation for, 133–135
    community engagement for, 137–141
    humor for, 136
    mind and body connection in, 125–129
    outdoor and nature time for, 129–131
    simplifying for, 124–125
    spirituality and religion for, 131–133
Standing Rock protest, 30–31
Staying, and stepping away, 145–146
Stepping away, 143–151
    and choice to escape with distractions,
        60
    and staying, 145–146
    vacation time in, 45–46
    walk away power in, 146–147
Stevenson, Bryan, 109, 131
Stewart, Jon, 75
Story, Colleen, 46
Stress
    animals reducing, 101–102
    economic, 47–48
    epigenetics in, 28–29
    from news, 77
    school-related, 44
Suicide, 15–16, 17, 31, 43, 93, 104, 132
Suzuki Roshi, 146
Syria, 116
Systematic oppression, 3, 31–34

T
Technology
    addiction to, 67, 68, 81, 96
    as distraction, 66–70, 80–83
    health effects of, 39–40
    intentional use of, 80–83
Terrorist attacks
    disconnection after, 90
    epigenetic effects of, 29
    intentional response after, 74–75
Tierney, John, 123
Toorpakai, Maria, 128–129
Trauma, 28
    epigenetics in, 28–29, 30
    intergenerational transmission of legacy,
        30–31
Tutu, Desmond, vii, 55, 84
Twenge, Jean, 39

V
Vacation time, international differences in,
    45–46
van der Kolk, Bessel, 19, 97
Vietor, Tommy, 111
Violence, community and society
    overwhelm from, 25
Voter registration campaign, 113–114
Vulnerability, feeling of, 59, 107–108

W
Walk away power, 146–147
Walker, Matthew, 36, 121
Ward, Adam, 13, 83, 93
Ward, Jay, 13–14, 83, 93–94
Warner, Colin, 83–84
Water supply, lead in, 23
Watts, Alan, 71
Whitman, Walt, 117
Wiesel, Elie, 154
Wilbur, Steven, 132
Williams, James, 82
Williams, Terry Tempest, 5
Winfrey, Oprah, 34
Wise, Eryn, 31
Wonder, Stevie, 55
Woodruff, Scott, 49
Workplace, 45–47
    attachment in, 103–104, 106, 113
    depletion in, 119–120
    disconnection in, 91, 93
    gratitude in, 83, 84
    information overload in, 46–47

Workplace, *continued*
    personal overwhelm in, 17
    staying in or stepping away from, 45–46,
        145–146, 147
    vacation time in, 45–46
World events, news of. *See* News of world
    events

X
Xu Hongci, 16

Y
Yarmuth, John, 24, 48
Yehuda, Rachel, 29
Yoga, 96–97

ABOUT THE AUTHOR

Laura van Dernoot Lipsky is the founding director of The Trauma Stewardship Institute and author of the best-selling book *Trauma Stewardship*. Widely recognized as a pioneer in the field of trauma exposure, she has worked with individuals, systems, and communities around the world for more than three decades.

Laura became one of the first to speak publicly on the connection between environmental science and trauma and the toll exacted on individuals and organizations as they witness mass extinctions, irreversible ecological losses, or other forms of human encroachment. Simultaneously, she has long been an activist engaged in movements for social and environmental justice, and has taught on issues surrounding systematic oppression and liberation theory. Her TED Talk—distilling some of the themes she shares to help people who have experienced human and environmental trauma find their way through—was one of the first to be delivered inside a women's correctional facility.

Laura is an advisor for several nonprofit boards, an associate producer of the award-winning film *A Lot Like You,* and was given a Yo! Mama award in recognition of her work as a community-activist mother.

Laura van Dernoot Lipsky with Connie Burk

Trauma Stewardship

An Everyday Guide to Caring for Self While Caring for Others

In this bestselling book, Laura van Dernoot Lipsky and Connie Burk offer a deep and empathetic survey of the often-unrecognized toll taken on those working to make the world a better place. We may feel tired, cynical, or numb or like we can never do enough. These and other symptoms affect us individually and collectively, sapping the energy and effectiveness we so desperately need if we are to benefit humankind, other living things, and the planet itself. In *Trauma Stewardship*, we are called to meet these challenges in an intentional way—to keep from becoming overwhelmed by developing a quality of mindful presence. Joining the wisdom of ancient cultural traditions with modern psychological research, Lipsky and Burk offer a variety of simple and profound practices that will allow us to remake ourselves—and ultimately the world.

288 pages, paperback, ISBN 978-1-57675-944-8
PDF ebook ISBN 978-1-60509-263-8
ePub ebook ISBN 978-1-60509-538-7
Digital audio ISBN 978-1-5230-9642-8

Berrett–Koehler Publishers, Inc.
www.bkconnection.com

800.929.2929

Berrett–Koehler
Publishers

Berrett-Koehler is an independent publisher dedicated to an ambitious mission: *Connecting people and ideas to create a world that works for all.*

We believe that the solutions to the world's problems will come from all of us, working at all levels: in our organizations, in our society, and in our own lives. Our BK Business books help people make their organizations more humane, democratic, diverse, and effective (we don't think there's any contradiction there). Our BK Currents books offer pathways to creating a more just, equitable, and sustainable society. Our BK Life books help people create positive change in their lives and align their personal practices with their aspirations for a better world.

All of our books are designed to bring people seeking positive change together around the ideas that empower them to see and shape the world in a new way.

And we strive to practice what we preach. At the core of our approach is Stewardship, a deep sense of responsibility to administer the company for the benefit of all of our stakeholder groups including authors, customers, employees, investors, service providers, and the communities and environment around us. Everything we do is built around this and our other key values of quality, partnership, inclusion, and sustainability.

This is why we are both a B-Corporation and a California Benefit Corporation—a certification and a for-profit legal status that require us to adhere to the highest standards for corporate, social, and environmental performance.

We are grateful to our readers, authors, and other friends of the company who consider themselves to be part of the BK Community. We hope that you, too, will join us in our mission.

A BK Life Book

BK Life books help people clarify and align their values, aspirations, and actions. Whether you want to manage your time more effectively or uncover your true purpose, these books are designed to instigate infectious positive change that starts with you. Make your mark!

To find out more, visit **www.bkconnection.com.**

Berrett–Koehler
Publishers

Connecting people and ideas
to create a world that works for all

Dear Reader,

Thank you for picking up this book and joining our worldwide community
of Berrett-Koehler readers. We share ideas that bring positive change into
people's lives, organizations, and society.

To welcome you, we'd like to offer you a free e-book. You can pick from
among twelve of our bestselling books by entering the promotional code
BKP92E here: http://www.bkconnection.com/welcome.

When you claim your free e-book, we'll also send you a copy of our e-news-
letter, the *BK Communiqué*. Although you're free to unsubscribe, there are
many benefits to sticking around. In every issue of our newsletter you'll find

- A free e-book
- Tips from famous authors
- Discounts on spotlight titles
- Hilarious insider publishing news
- A chance to win a prize for answering a riddle

Best of all, our readers tell us, "Your newsletter is the only one I actually
read." So claim your gift today, and please stay in touch!

Sincerely,

Charlotte Ashlock
Steward of the BK Website

Questions? Comments? Contact me at bkcommunity@bkpub.com.

MIX
Paper from
responsible sources
FSC® C016245
www.fsc.org

Certified
B
Corporation
bcorporation.net